ESSENTIAL PSYCHOLOGY

General Editor
Peter Herriot

A4

PERCEPTION AND INFORMATION

ESSENTIAL

PSYCHOLOGY

PERCEPTION
AND
INFORMATION

**Paul J. Barber and
David Legge**

Methuen

First published in 1976 by Methuen & Co Ltd
11 New Fetter Lane, London EC4P 4EE
© 1976 Paul J. Barber and David Legge
Printed in Great Britain by
Richard Clay (The Chaucer Press), Ltd
Bungay, Suffolk

ISBN (hardback) 0 416 82030 1
ISBN (paperback) 0 416 82040 9

We are grateful to Grant McIntyre of Open Books Publishing Ltd
for assistance in the preparation of this series.

Contents

Preface

Perception is about receiving, selecting, acquiring, transforming and organizing the information supplied through our senses. It is about vision, hearing, smell, taste, touch, and more. But this maps out an immense territory and we have competence and space to examine only a small selection of the related topics and issues.

Introducing perception is a bit like describing a banquet. One way would be to give the menu – but this doesn't tell you what the cooking is like and, in any case, the 'best' menus are written for gourmets in unreadable French. One might alternatively think of asking the Chef, but the channels of communication have so far proved elusive!

Our solution is, therefore, to give a sample of some of the dishes – though hopefully not so many that the flavour is of a bland unmemorable tapioca pudding. We could have tried to convey the essence of the perceptual banquet by offering a range of *hors-d'œuvre* but have instead decided that it can best be represented by the inclusion of a few main courses as well. Mother's advice not to bolt one's food is intended to avoid indigestion – it also brings out the flavour. We endorse it!

We thank Patricia Caple for typing the recipes, and Vicky Barber for typing and illustrating them.

7

Editor's Introduction

How much do we see out of the corner of our eye? Can we attend to more than one thing at the same time? Do we recognize the features of something before we actually identify it? Why are we deceived by visual illusions? Paul Barber and David Legge ask and try to answer these and other questions. They pose a yet more crucial question – to what extent do the laboratory methods we have used hitherto to investigate perception bear any relation to the daily tasks of looking and listening?

This book belongs to Unit A of *Essential Psychology*. What unifies the titles in this unit is the notion of the human being as a processor of information. Like a computer we can register information, code it, perform operations on the coded version, store the result, and subsequently retrieve it. Moreover, like a computer, we can use our output, or behaviour, as feedback or evidence by which to monitor our subsequent performance. The authors in Unit A are more concerned with making generalizations about people than with exploring their individual differences. Further, they deal with personal mental processes rather than with interpersonal social processes. They also probably place more stress on the traditional scientific experiment as a source of evidence than do most of the authors of the other units. However, the computer analogy may not be suitable for handling other situations, where there is no immediate sensory experience or no easily identifiable consequent behaviour. And some psychologists also feel that it detracts from the concept of the individual as a person who can consciously act upon and control his environment. The reader will find other general conceptual frameworks in other units. Psychology is struggling to do justice to the complexities of its subject matter; it is hardly likely to find any single analogy to encompass the richness of human behaviour and experience. Coming to terms with a variety of explanatory frameworks may decrease our confidence in psychology as a mature science; but perhaps it is best that we should be honest about what we don't know.

Essential Psychology as a whole is designed to reflect the changing structure and function of psychology. The authors are both academics and professionals, and their aim has been to introduce the most important concepts in their areas to beginning students. They have tried to do so clearly, but have not attempted to conceal the fact that concepts that now appear central to their work may soon be peripheral. In other words, they have presented psychology as a developing set of views of man, not as a body of received truth. Readers are not intended to study the whole series in order to 'master the basics'. Rather, since different people may wish to use different theoretical frameworks for their own purposes, the series has been designed so that each title stands on its own. But it is possible that if the reader has read no psychology before, he will enjoy individual books more if he has read the introductions (A1, B1, etc.) to the units to which they belong. Readers of the units concerned with applications of psychology (E and F) may benefit from reading all the introductions.

A word about references in the text to the work of other writers – e.g. 'Smith, 1974'. These occur where the author feels he must acknowledge (by name) an important concept or some crucial evidence. The book or article referred to will be listed in the references (which double as name index) at the back of the book. The reader is invited to consult these sources if he wishes to explore topics further. A list of general further reading is also to be found at the back of this book.

We hope you enjoy psychology.

Peter Herriot

1
Some preliminaries

Dark adaptation: a problem for perception psychology?

A familiar experience is that of entering a dark room after being exposed to bright sunlight. A similar one is of entering a cinema or theatre when the lights have gone down. Initially we seem to have very little sight – and we find our way about with some difficulty. Not much time has to elapse, a matter of a minute or so, before the lighting conditions seem to improve. After several minutes the change is quite dramatic and we can see about us reasonably clearly, at least to the extent of being able to see much more detail than before.

It will probably be readily accepted that it is not the lighting conditions that have changed, but to be sure about this we need independent verification. If we are in a cinema or theatre we could get an answer by asking our neighbours. This would be a satisfactory approach although it is guaranteed to lower our social desirability rating by a degree or so. By this, or the more sophisticated method of taking physical measurements of the illumination level, we could easily confirm that the change was in us. The effect is so compelling that it seems to call for a psychological explanation. This phenomenon is called *dark adaptation* and it will be used to introduce the study of perception and its methods. Let us see how we could discover more about dark adaptation, and perhaps move some way towards an explanation.

Verbal reports are one of the important sources of data in perception, as in other branches of psychology. They serve as a springboard for more systematic investigations of some phenomena, but may be the object of study in their own right. We might begin our investigation of dark adaptation by persuading some other individuals to act as observers and to give us verbal descriptions of the phenomenon. Their reported experience would confirm that dark adaptation is to do with an increase in sensitivity to light, that it is progressive, but also that it reaches some kind of limit. That is, we don't go on becoming more and more sensitive indefinitely. According to reports, then, sensitivity to light is initially very low, improves quite rapidly to begin with, but ultimately reaches a steady level. Incidentally, at the end of this 'descriptive experiment' we shall encounter the opposite process, of light adaptation, if we go from the dark into a well-lit environment.

It is unlikely that much will be learned from verbal description about the *form* of the relation between sensitivity and the duration of exposure to the dark, and we shall have to use a more precise procedure for estimating sensitivity. Verbal reports may nevertheless be informative in other ways. For example, an observer might say that he heard a ticking sound that speeded up according to the visibility of the surrounding objects. We are quite certain that no observer would make *this* particular statement (at least we hope so!), but it is this kind of information that the verbal report method supplies that can lead to insights about explanations (see also p. 18).

More precise data about dark adaptation could be obtained with the use of one of the *psychophysical methods*. They were developed in the nineteenth century for the purpose of estimating how *psycho*logical variables were linked with *physical* ones. In the present case we are talking about sensitivity to light and this could be measured more precisely as the least amount of light energy the observer could see: this quantity is known as the *absolute threshold* for vision.

One way of estimating the absolute threshold is to present to the observer a series of lights whose intensities vary in small steps ranging from values that he can see to those that he cannot. The entirely crucial thing about this range of values is that it should contain the threshold. Various economies of time and effort and other considerations (e.g. that the observer is not sent to sleep) dictate that a truncated range is used in practice. On a particular occasion or *trial*, the

12

subject (or 'observer' as we shall often call him) is asked to say 'yes' if he can see the *stimulus* (the light in this case) but to say 'no' otherwise. According to the *ascending method of limits* the light intensities are presented in increasing order until the limiting point is reached when the subject says 'yes'; the light intensity or luminance at this point can be taken at his threshold.

Since we are taking pains over the measurement of sensitivity it will be sensible for us to take the experiment to a laboratory with black-out facilities, and which provides a quiet undistracting environment. In the course of familiarizing ourselves with the experimental procedure we are likely to discover some intriguing characteristics of the threshold. It varies from trial to trial, not just on account of dark adaptation since the variations (which are upwards as well as downwards) also occur in fully dark-adapted observers. It is not a fixed quantity for a given observer, and it also varies from individual to individual. Furthermore, if instead of stopping the series of trials as soon as the subject reported seeing the stimulus we continued increasing the intensity, it is quite possible that he would report no light on the next trial. A typical series of responses as the intensity level increases is shown in Table 1.1 (no significance is to be attached to the actual intensity values used):

Table 1.1 Sample record of observer's responses in a threshold experiment

Stimulus intensity level (arbitrary units)													
12	13	14	15	16	17	18	19	20	21	22	23	24	25
Response No	No	No	No	No	Yes	No	No	Yes	No	Yes	Yes	Yes	Yes

In the face of this kind of variability it is left to the experimenter to define the threshold himself. The decision is an arbitrary one forced on him by the instability of the responses. Steps can be taken to obtain as 'pure' a measure as possible (avoiding distraction; making sure the equipment performs without error; keeping the subject's interest, attention and bodily state as constant as possible) but there is almost inevitably some change in the 'threshold' value from trial to trial. In Table 1.1 some of the options are to take 16·5 (midway between the first 'yes' and preceding 'no'), or 21·5 (between the first of two successive 'yeses' and the preceding 'no'). In practice several estimates of the visual threshold, however defined, are likely to be obtained and their average value taken as the threshold.

The dark adaptation experiment is now almost ready to begin, but subjects still have to be recruited and instructed. It will be as well not to ask people to come along immediately after eating a large meal, playing squash or drinking eight pints of beer (unless of course we are interested in the effects of eating, exercise or drinking on dark adaptation). We shall also be well advised to arrange for their initial state of light adaptation to be effectively standardized; before the experiment, therefore, they should be asked to inspect a brightly illuminated screen for a prescribed interval.

Care has to be taken over the instructions, not only to make them comprehensible, but to arrange that the subject maintains the same definition or criterion of what constitutes a stimulus throughout the experiment. It will not serve our purpose if he sets out saying 'yes' whenever the merest hint of a stimulus is seen, and then later in the session he demands much more evidence before responding. Even in a simple situation like the absolute threshold procedure the subject's criterion for responding may affect the estimated value of the threshold; a cautious or conservative approach to the task leads to a high threshold, while a low value will be obtained if a risky or liberal criterion is used.

Next we have to accept a compromise between these efforts at methodological rigour and the object of the exercise – which after this detour may need repeating – namely, to plot the course of dark adaptation. The problem is that we cannot afford to take multiple measurements of the threshold. It takes time to get a single threshold measurement and while this is being done the state of dark adaptation may well be changing; so what was not perceptible thirty seconds ago may well be now. The procedure itself must be adapted to suit the urgency of the circumstances. We may decide on a single ascending series of stimuli presented with a reasonably brief interval between them. A case could even be made for the rather free-wheeling *method of adjustment* in which the presentation of the stimulus is handed over to the subject, typically involving the use of a continuous control of the stimulus intensity (like the volume control on a radio or record player); the method is a bit sloppy because the experimenter no longer has control over which stimulus values are presented or their rate of presentation. A pilot study will be needed to suggest what range of stimulus values should be used, and this range will have to be shifted downwards in the course of the dark adaptation session.

The final consideration concerns the apparatus we shall need for obtaining a range of light intensities. On the face of it all we need is a way of varying the current to a small lamp placed at the back of a translucent screen. A device like a household dimmer switch would be appropriate for this, but anyone who has seen the effect produced on an ordinary tungsten filament lamp will know that the variation in current produced by twiddling the dimmer switch is accompanied not only by a change in light intensity but also by a change in the hue of the light. At high intensities it is yellow-white but at low intensities it is quite noticeably reddish. This change in hue results from a change in the wavelength of the light emitted by the lamp. Clearly we don't want to do an experiment in which intensity and hue vary at the same time. This 'confounding' of the two variables (see A8) can be avoided by using a special light source like an electroluminescent panel, or by moving the lamp relative to a screen on which it is projecting its light; the latter method ensures that the wavelength is constant but by changing the distance between source and screen the amount of energy falling on the screen can be systematically varied.

Having been battered with all these cautions and qualifications, the reader may be nervously waiting for another trap to be sprung. However, the dirty tricks department of the perceptual system has had its say for the moment and we promise little more than a (slightly) surprise ending. The point of all this is that similar considerations crop up in the course of all perceptual investigations, and as might be expected the problems are no less knotty if we are dealing with complicated processes like searching for needles in haystacks, watching radar screens, deciphering morse code, reading, recognizing somebody's voice, wine-tasting, discriminating between margarine and butter and so on.

Figure 1.1 presents a schematic version of the kind of data we could reasonably expect to emerge from our experiment, using a violet light as the stimulus. As we suspected there is a rapid decrease in the threshold – signifying an increase in sensitivity – over the first few minutes of exposure to the dark, and after half an hour or so it reaches a more or less steady state. But quite unexpectedly there is a kink in the curve when the subject has been in the dark for around ten minutes. The double-scalloped look of this curve suggests that dark adaptation is not a unitary process, and that it might be sensible to look for a pair of underlying mechanisms. Further investigation would reveal that the threshold-

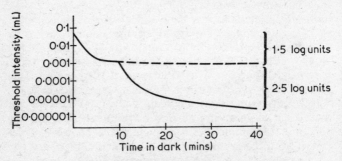

Fig. 1.1 *Dark adaptation: absolute visual threshold as a function of time in darkness*

time relation is sensitive to properties of the stimulus, like its hue (which justifies our caution about the method of varying light intensity) and the intensity of the level of illumination to which the subject had previously been exposed (called the 'adapting field').

More detailed study gives a hint that the mechanisms responsible for dark adaptation may not be buried deep inside the nervous system but may be found in the eye, that furthest outpost of the brain. In order to come closer to an explanation of dark adaptation a further detour is called for; this will involve a cursory examination of some aspects of the anatomy and physiology of the eye.

The eye (Fig. 1.2) is about 1 inch in diameter and is protected in front by the transparent *cornea* and otherwise by a tough opaque membrane called the *sclera* (this protrudes to the front of the eye and is what we call the white of the eye). Light enters the eye via the pupil which is a gap in the *iris*, the muscular structure covering part of the lens which gives the eye its colour. Beyond the iris is the *lens* which does the job of focusing light on the retina.

The *retina* is the thin layer at the back of the eye which contains about 130 million light-sensitive receptors whose

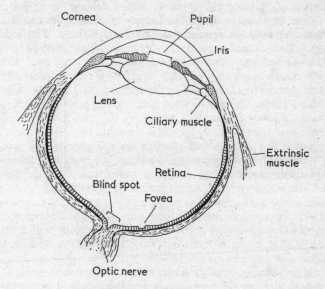

Fig. 1.2 *The human eye*

activity is transmitted via a bundle of nerves forming the *optic fibre* to the brain. At the centre of the retina the sheet of receptors is thinnest and this small region is known as the *fovea*. It turns out to have distinctive properties, one of which is demonstrated in dark adaptation. If the stimulus is a red light or is directed at the fovea only, then the dark adaptation curve loses its kink and proceeds as shown by the dotted line in Figure 1.1. It appears that the two parts of the dark adaptation curve may be linked to some difference between the fovea and the outer region or periphery of the retina. The kink in the curve can also be eliminated by using a low level of illumination for the adapting field.

The retinal layer consists of an intricate arrangement of *photoreceptors* and their associated neural circuitry. The ingredients of this thin structure turn out to be more or less directly responsible for the phenomena we have described. The receptors of the visual system are located here and they form two classes, the *rods* and the *cones*, so-called because of their shapes. The distribution of rods and cones across the retina is of particular interest. The 7 million or so cones cluster predominantly in the foveal region and become less and less frequent further out into the periphery. The rods are much more numerous: there are approximately 120 million of them. They are not found in the fovea and, with one qualification, they increase rapidly to a maximum density and then decrease steadily to the furthest periphery at about 100 degrees. The qualification concerns the *blind spot* which is the zone where nearly 1 million nerve fibres gather in the course of leaving the eye to form the optic fibre. This region spans a few degrees and contains no receptors of any sort.

The evidence is beginning to add up. We have an anatomical distinction between the fovea (cones only) and the rest of the retina (mainly rods). We also know that the second dip in the dark adaptation curve fails to appear if the light is carefully projected onto the fovea only. The double-scalloped dark adaptation curve seems to be related to some functional distinction between rods and cones, presumably reflecting their different sensitivities to light.

The rods are indeed more sensitive than the cones, as shown in Figure 1.3 by their lower thresholds at all wavelengths except at the red end of the spectrum. The U-shaped form of this graph shows how sensitivity falls off at the red and violet extremes of the spectrum where a more intense light is needed to reach threshold than for intermediate wavelengths.

The kink in the dark adaptation curve in Figure 1.1 showed where the cones were maximally sensitized, and the second dip was the result of the continuing increase in sensitivity of the rods. The verbal report of the observer would also reflect this changeover: before the kink he would say that the test stimulus was blue but after that it would look colourless. This reflects another difference between rod and cone vision: only the cones are involved in colour perception.

From Figure 1.3 it can also be seen why the use of red light removed the kink from the dark adaptation curve. The rods went on adapting as usual but their increased general sensitivity no longer showed up because the stimulus used was from a specific region where their sensitivity is poorest. This is put to use by aircraft pilots flying at night, who need to dark-adapt before take-off. If dark red goggles are worn

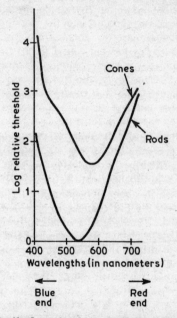

Fig . 1.3 *Absolute visual thresholds as a function of wavelength for rod and cone vision*

then the individual can still see enough via cone vision to find his way about in normal lighting conditions, but at the same time he prevents his rods from light-adapting. In this way the rods are kept maximally sensitive to the rest of the spectrum.

Dark adaptation is one facet of the ability of the visual system to respond to any of a huge range of stimulus intensities. Measured in the most common unit of light intensity, the millilambert (mL), this range of luminances is from about

0.000001 or 10^{-6} mL at absolute threshold to about 1 million or 10^6 mL at the tolerance threshold. The latter refers to the highest luminance to which the eye responds; it is at this end of the range that damage to the eye is possible. This corresponds to a range of responsiveness in which the largest intensity is 10^{12} or a billion times greater than the smallest. The variation in pupil size – like the variation in the iris diaphragm of a camera – can produce a mere ten- to twentyfold change in sensitivity, so the remainder is accounted for by changes elsewhere in the visual system. The comparable range of responsiveness in a good camera with several 'f-stops' is unlikely to be more than 1,000 : 1. The camera's effectiveness is enhanced by using films of different sensitivity or 'speed'. This is also achieved by the retina, but in effect by varying the film speed without changing the film.

With such uncomfortably large numbers of zeros it will be appreciated that the use of logarithmic units is often preferred; in these terms the range is 12 log units. However, there is only generally about a 2 log unit variation in the luminances confronting us, and our working range of responsiveness is a lot smaller than the one just referred to. This working range shifts about depending on the visual circumstances, as we see by the changes in the lower limit of responsiveness in dark (and light) adaptation. In dark adaptation the cones mediate a change in sensitivity of about 1·5 units, while the rods continue this operation for a further 2·5 log units; in the course of forty minutes there is a gain in sensitivity of 4 log units, i.e. the threshold at the end of the session is 10,000 times lower than at the outset. The dark adaptation process seems to offer us a perceptual facility analogous to the volume control knob on a radio which we adjust according to the strength of the signal.

The slow course of dark adaptation presumably has some evolutionary background. No doubt if there had been a kind of prehistoric Hollywood our visual systems would have developed a little differently. As it is they cause us little inconvenience short of the occasional stubbed toe or uninvited social encounter when the lights go down.

The comparative slowness of dark adaptation is a reflection of its chemical origins in the retina. When light energy collides with a rod (its mechanism is better understood than that of the cones) a chemical reaction takes place in which a light-sensitive substance or photopigment called *rhodopsin* is involved. This in turn serves to trigger a neural signal from the rod. The absorption of light results in the bleaching, or loss of pigment, in the rhodopsin. A restorative process then acts to bring the rhodopsin content back to its previous level; this is a slow process, taking about forty minutes or so to complete.

It was considered for some time that dark adaptation was the result solely of the regeneration of rhodopsin, and this is supported by the comparable time courses of sensitivity changes and rhodopsin levels. At the same time light adaptation was thought to be due to the bleaching process. But there are findings that suggest that this is not the whole story. Visual thresholds can change quite rapidly even though the rhodopsin content is stable and the speed of these changes suggests that a neural mechanism must also be involved.

With a little help from our friends, the physiologists and anatomists, we have tracked the dark adaptation process down to its very origins. As we agreed it certainly is not the lighting conditions that change when we lose vision on being plunged into darkness. The factors responsible for this and the subsequent recovery of vision are contained in the retina – as we recognize when we say 'my eyes have got used to the dark'. This turns out to be surprisingly close to the mark. There are few other perceptual phenomena that can be so firmly attributed to an underlying structural state of affairs and we shall not often again in this book be able to shift the level of explanation as far as this.

2
Structure and beyond

Peripheral vision

What can be seen with 'the corner of one's eye' is limited. Visual acuity in the periphery is poor and detailed inspection of an object generally entails bringing the foveal region of the retina to bear on it. Duly cautioned by our discovery of the importance of the retinal hardware we could hypothesize that this was a result of the 'duplex' nature of the retina. Our discussion, therefore, continues with the properties of peripheral vision and its role in a variety of perceptual tasks.

The resolving power of the eye, or *visual acuity*, is measured by the familiar Snellen chart of the optician. Other methods include the measurement of the smallest detectable gap in a figure like that of Figure 2.1(a), the smallest resolvable interval between bars of a grating like Figure 2.1(b), and the least detectable misalignment of a pair of lines as in Figure 2.1(c). Visual acuity, as measured by these techniques, depends quite critically on the retinal location used. It is best in the fovea, thereafter decreasing very rapidly to become poorest in the extreme periphery. The rate of decrease is quite remarkable over the first 1 or 2 degrees of visual angle, but is more gradual thereafter. The angle involved can be judged from the fact that a ten-letter word in this book can just about be accommodated within a visual angle of 2 degrees if the reading distance is 30 cm.

The rapid drop in acuity corresponds to the transition from foveal to peripheral or extrafoveal vision. In the fovea acuity is greatest where the cones are most densely crowded together. In the retinal circuitry the cones are connected to neurons called bipolar cells in a one-to-one fashion, while several rods connect to a given bipolar. These connections are shown schematically in Figure 2.2. As a consequence

(a) Landolt Cs: the observer has to report the orientation of the gap.

(b) Resolution grating: at a long distance from the eye the grating is seen as a matte grey but at a short distance the lines can be distinguished (resolved).

(c) Vernier acuity: the separation between the lines is adjusted until they appear to be in alignment.

Fig. 2.1 *Visual acuity tasks*

the rods, for all their greater sensitivity to light *per se*, are less well equipped for the acuity task. Nevertheless, because of their poor sensitivity at low luminance levels the cones do not then maintain their high acuity capability; so acuity is very poor at low luminances, being mainly mediated by the rods.

A behavioural result of the rod-cone difference in receptor-neuron connections is the phenomenon of *spatial summation*: the absolute threshold intensity obtained in the dark-adapted periphery is independent of the size of the spot of light used provided it does not exceed ten minutes of arc. There is very little spatial summation in the fovea. This suggests a qualitative difference in the information that can be extracted by the rods and cones.

It seems to follow from this that peripheral vision is useless for tasks requiring fine detail, like the identification of forms or shapes. Early experiments, in which observers were asked to give the names of forms (circles, squares, triangles and the like), confirmed that performance at this kind of task indeed fell off rapidly as the forms were taken out into the periphery.

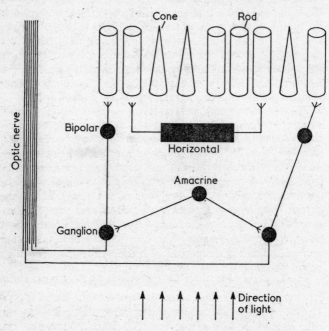

Fig. 2.2 *Schematic diagram of the retinal layer, showing main interconnections between receptors and neurons*

NOTE: The direction of the light on the retina is from bottom to top in this diagram, with the photoreceptors at the top. Light in fact has to penetrate a thicket of neurons, blood vessels and nerve bodies and a large proportion of the light energy is lost without reaching the rods and cones.

Recent evidence, however, has tended to controvert the earlier studies at least in the sense of suggesting that peripheral visual competence has been underestimated. We shall examine some of this evidence in detail. This will lead to a discussion of much more complex perceptual processes.

The proposition that the effectiveness of form perception in peripheral vision is greater than was previously believed is supported by an experiment by Menzer and Thurmond (1970). A collection of specially constructed forms was used: polygons formed by making random connections between points and figures like bar charts also constructed on a random basis. On any trial one of these (the target) could be placed in the periphery at any one of a series of angles (5, 20, 35, 50, 65 and 80 degrees). For a man looking squarely at a point on a flat wall 2 feet away, these angles correspond to distances to the side of his fixation point of approximately 0·2, 0·7, 1·4, 2·4, 4·3 and 11·3 feet. Ahead of the observer (at 0 degrees visual angle) were three figures, including a blank square.

The observer's task was to indicate via the choice forms what he considered was being shown to him in the periphery. If there was no form he was to select the blank square, but if there was then he was to choose one of the two other forms. These three alternatives were each correct on one-third of the trials and so if he responded purely by guesswork he would be correct coincidentally 33 per cent of the time; this is the chance baseline against which his performance can be compared. To be sure that the observer was looking where he was instructed the movements of his eyes were recorded. The last important detail of the procedure is that the forms were either 'solid' (painted black) or drawn in 'outline'.

Performance, measured as the percentage of correct responses for each class of form, decreased as the target moved further out into the periphery, but there was a sharper decline for outline forms from about 20 degrees outwards. The level of performance was well above the chance score except at 80 degrees; even this far into the periphery, performance on solid polygons was as high as 63 per cent. The comparative advantage to solid forms in the periphery was predicted on the basis of the spatial summation property of the rods. The findings reinforce the suggestion that the periphery processes information in a qualitatively distinct way to the fovea.

Consider what happens in reading, and what role the periphery might have. Outside the fovea the text has a fuzzy appearance and the question is whether this perceptual blur is any material use in reading. If the acuity results are to be relied upon, the fovea could be thought of as the beam of a torch illuminating a small region of text. This foveal spotlight does not make a smooth continuous scan and its progress is marked by momentary pauses (fixations) and rapid jumps (eye movements) to a new piece of text. What information is used in 'deciding' where to fixate next? Of course we don't carry out calculations of which we are even indirectly aware but in some sense a 'decision' is made somewhere in the nervous system about where to look next. Conceivably it is in part based on information acquired via the extrafoveal retina. Evidence relating to the torchbeam analogy is discussed in Chapter 4. Meantime we shall move on to a theoretical initiative based on some experiments on the ease of distinguishing between stimuli viewed extrafoveally. First, however, we have to take a small but important detour.

Principles of perceptual organization

One of the most significant contributions to the study of perception was made by a group of psychologists who formed the Gestalt school of thought, most active and influential in the first half of this century. One of its members, Wertheimer, claimed that we do not perceive objects as an accumulation of isolated sensations, but as organized wholes, or *Gestalten*.

I stand at the window and see a house, trees, sky. Now on theoretical grounds I could try to count and say: 'Here there are ... 327 brightnesses and hues.' Do I have '327'? No, I see sky, house, trees; and no one can really have these '327' as such. (Wertheimer, 1958)

Examples of this organization are given in Figure 2.3. These demonstrations were collected together and rather misleadingly referred to as 'principles' or 'laws' of perceptual organization. Figure 2.3 shows three kinds of perceptual grouping.

According to the *proximity principle* elements which are close together are perceived as a group. Thus in Figure 2.3(a) one sees five columns of dots rather than five rows. *Similarity grouping* is demonstrated by Figure 2.3(b) in which rows of dots alternating with rows of crosses are seen, not columns of dots and crosses intermingled. Figure 2.3(c) is typically seen as two series of dots crossing, and not as a V-shape in conjunction with an inverted V-shape; this illustrates *good con-*

tinuation. In each case the mentioned alternative is usually difficult to see. These 'principles' are of long standing but have not been given much experimental scrutiny. Prominent amongst the research that has been conducted is a series of experiments considered in the next section; this serves also to return us to the question of peripheral vision.

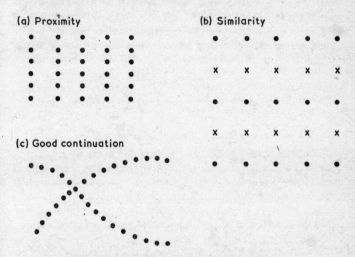

Fig. 2.3 *Examples of perceptual grouping*

Grouping and peripheral discriminability

The demonstrations in Figure 2.3 have intuitive appeal, and indeed they may seem so obvious that it is not clear that there is anything to explain; although the difficulty of achieving an alternative percept in each case suggests otherwise. The problem is that it is hard to state what stimulus properties are involved. Beck (1966) set out to remedy this situation for the particular case of similarity grouping. He used displays that consisted of two kinds of elements (e.g. Ts and upside-down Ts, or Ts and sloping Ts) like those in Figure 2.4. The subject had merely to say whether or not they formed groups. The display apparatus enabled the luminance of one set to be adjusted so that one set was brighter than the other. Beck found that there had to be a bigger discrepancy in the luminances if the inverted Ts were to be seen as grouped;

grouping was easier when the second set were sloping.

Grouping was in general more elusive if the transformation from the basic figure left the component lines horizontal and vertical (as in a 90 degree or 180 degree rotation). This was confirmed in other experiments in which the number of elements had to be counted, and also when a subjective judgement using a scale of numbers was made of how well segregated the two classes were.

Line slope seems to be one of the stimulus properties that leads to grouping. Further research has shown that the same stimulus property is connected with ease of discrimination in

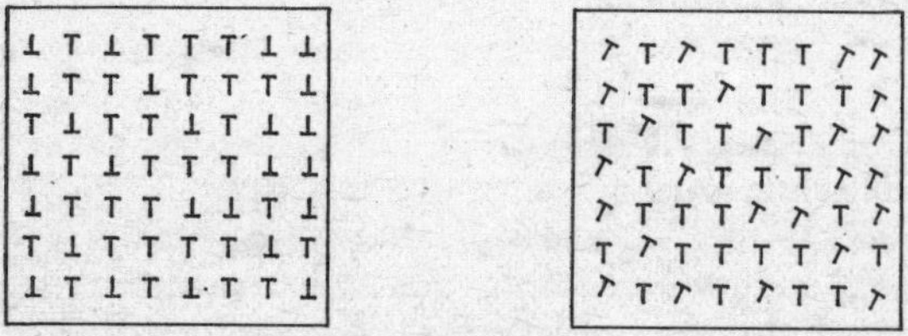

```
⊥ T ⊥ T T T ⊥ ⊥          ⼂ T ⼂ T T T ⼂ ⼂
⊥ T T ⊥ T T T ⊥          ⼂ T T ⼂ T T T ⼂
T ⊥ T T ⊥ T ⊥ ⊥          T ⼂ T T ⼂ T ⼂ ⼂
⊥ T ⊥ T T T ⊥ ⊥          ⼂ T ⼂ T T T ⼂ ⼂
⊥ T T T ⊥ ⊥ T ⊥          ⼂ T T T ⼂ ⼂ T ⼂
T ⊥ T T T T ⊥ T          T ⼂ T T T T ⼂ T
⊥ T ⊥ T ⊥ T T ⊥          ⼂ T ⼂ T ⼂ T T ⼂
```

Fig. 2.4 *Similarity grouping and line orientation (after Beck, 1966)*

peripheral vision. That is, figures which differ in line slope (e.g. upright and sloping T) are easier to distinguish from one another than figures which differ in line arrangement (e.g. upright and inverted T). This result was found with a task in which four figures were shown peripherally and one of them (the target) differed from the others in line slope or line arrangement; the subject had to indicate the nature of the odd-man-out. But it did not apply when the target stimulus was presented on its own and the other three possible locations were empty (Beck, 1972).

This complication is revealing because it suggests that the line slope property is effective even when attention has to be distributed evenly over the display. When there is an opportunity to focus attention on the target the line arrangement differences can be picked up equally well. Certain stimulus properties, which include size and brightness, seem to be signalled quite effectively via the periphery, and it is possible that they may be useful in the guidance of attention.

So we have hinted at some new theoretical concepts and

questions. The discussion has continued to be organized around the question of peripheral vision, but it will be apparent that we have increasingly needed to resort to concepts of a more complicated kind that implicate the working of systems much deeper in the brain, while being quite indefinite about their physiological location or likely structure. This is entirely typical of the psychology of perception. We continue our journey through the visual system by returning to our survey of the retinal layers.

Retinal structure

The signals generated by the rods and cones in response to light are transmitted to a layer of bipolar cells. The neural impulse is then passed to one of the *ganglion cells*, which collectively form the optic fibre, leaving the eye at the blind spot. This circuitry is shown schematically in Figure 2.2. There are further 'sideways' or lateral connections with the *horizontal* and *amacrine cells*. The importance of this lateral network is that it enables stimulation at one part of the retina to influence activity at a second site. What lateral influences are exerted in the human retina are not known directly. However, the much simpler and more accessible eyes of certain animals have been very thoroughly investigated, and have provided insights into the kinds of processing that might be carried out by the human visual system.

Lateral inhibition: through the eye of the limulus

One of these animals is the horseshoe-crab, or limulus. It is a comparatively straightforward matter to stimulate an individual receptor of the limulus eye with light, something which is hard to guarantee in the intact human eye. The electrical response of this receptor can be studied by placing a microelectrode (see A2) at the ganglion cell fed by the receptor. The evidence about the limulus eye has suggested some likely mechanisms for the extraction of information that could underly the perception of brightness and form.

One of the most important of these is *lateral inhibition* (Ratliff, 1972), illustrated by Figure 2.5. Suppose the output of a receptor A is recorded in response to a light. In the absence of the light there will typically be a small spontaneous discharge from its associated ganglion cell as shown by the infrequent bars or 'spikes' in Figure 2.5(a). When the light is turned on the rate of firing increases considerably and then generally reverts to a steady rate. Now consider what happens when an evidently isolated but adjacent receptor B is stimulated. The ganglion cell at A shows no change in the spontaneous rate of firing (Fig. 2.5(b)). Finally, let both receptors be stimulated,

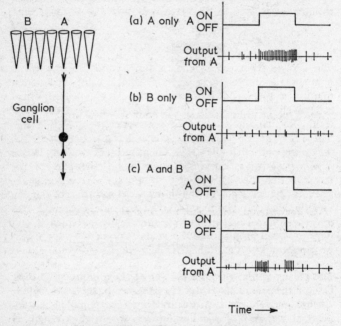

Fig. 2.5 *Illustration of lateral inhibition*

A first and then B, and it is found that the firing of A decreases when B is stimulated and it recovers when the light at B is again turned off (Fig. 2.5(c)).

The receptor at B has an inhibitory effect on its nearby companion, and closer inspection would reveal the lateral fibres mediating this effect. Models of a mathematical kind have been constructed to simulate the lateral inhibition effect with some success. Quite a simple mechanism of this sort can in principle produce interesting effects at boundaries between light and dark zones which correspond to a slight enhancement of the contour.

Brightness contrast
A phenomenon that has also been connected with lateral inhibition is *simultaneous brightness contrast*, demonstrated in Figure 2.6. The two central squares are in fact of an identical grey and therefore reflect the same amount of light, and yet the square on the black background is brighter than

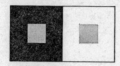

(a) The two central squares are of an identical grey.

(b) Background rectangles for contrast demonstration (see text).

Fig. 2.6 *Simultaneous brightness contrast*

that on the white background. The effect is more compelling if the viewer can interchange the squares: panel (b) of Figure 2.6 can be used for this purpose. Two small pieces of grey paper should be placed one on each sector of the rectangle. If grey paper is not available then any pale pastel colour will serve the purpose – the matte inside surface of a manilla envelope is ideal. Moving the two pieces of paper about relative to their border, interchanging them and moving a desk lamp towards the page enable contrast effects to be explored.

A more dramatic effect which has been discussed in terms of contrast is an effect described by Gelb in 1929. An observer in an otherwise completely dark room sees a disc covered with black velvet and rotating fast (to ensure a homogeneous surface), and illuminated by a spotlight, so precisely in fact that there is no stray light. This disc appears to be white. But now a small piece of white paper is placed in front of the disc, which instantaneously appears to be darker. As soon as the white paper is removed the disc looks white again. This effect seems to involve brightness contrast but a complete explanation will probably be more involved than this.

The basic contrast effect seems to be related to lateral inhibition. This mechanism can serve to accentuate the differences in intensity on either side of a dark-light boundary. A white surround will have an inhibitory effect on the neural output corresponding to the grey square, and a black surround will have an enhancement effect. But although this may account for the effects at the edges it also has to be explained why the effect extends through the affected grey regions.

Visual pathways

The retinal signals arising from an external stimulus are transformed at a number of stages on their way through the visual system. First we consider their route to the visual cortex (Fig. 2.7) – the cortex is the collection of cells forming the peculiar convoluted grey surface layer of the brain (see A2).

Nerve fibres originating in the half of the retina nearer the nose travel to the opposite or *contralateral* hemisphere of the cortex, while those emanating from the half nearer the temple go to the corresponding, or *ipsilateral*, hemisphere. The crossover occurs in the optic chiasm (not shown in Fig. 2.7).

Both eyes are thus connected to both cerebral hemispheres, but the route is such that the left and right halves of the object (stimulus) map to the right and left hemispheres respectively. However, the left-most parts of the object will only fall on the nasal half-retina of the left eye, so that they are only represented in the right visual cortex via the crossed fibres from the left eye. Similarly the right-most parts are represented only via the nasal half-retina of the right eye.

The optic fibre terminates prior to the cortex in a structure called the *lateral geniculate nucleus* (LGN) where the individual nerves have their first synaptic connection after the retina. The LGN, a kind of half-way house which has been closely studied by physiologists, projects onto the visual or striate area of the cortex. There are also pathways linking both the optic nerves and the visual cortex with a midbrain structure known as the *superior colliculus*, but little is known about the role in vision of this and related structures.

In the retinal layer a given ganglion cell may be the recipient of signals from many rods or a single cone. The retinal

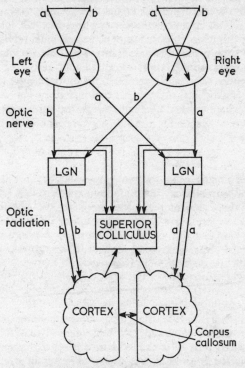

LGN = Lateral geniculate nucleus

Fig. 2.7 *Schematic diagram of the visual pathways in man*

For convenience the stimulus 'ab' is shown represented separately for the two eyes. Notice that 'a' on the left of the object is registered in the right visual cortex in pathways from both eyes.

area which maps onto a given ganglion cell is its *receptive field*, generally organized as a pair of concentric circles. In some cases stimulation of the central area increases the rate of firing while stimulation of the surrounding area decreases it; for obvious reasons these are called centre-on/surround-off cells.

This is like the lateral inhibition arrangement considered above. A second kind of receptive field organization is known as centre-off/surround-on, with activity triggered by a stimulus to the outer ring and inhibited by one to the central area.

Receptive field organization has also been investigated for cells in the lateral geniculate bodies and beyond, to points well into the visual cortex in the cat and monkey. An intriguing aspect of this research is that it demonstrates a neural representation of certain stimulus properties, as indicated by the shape and nature of receptive fields. For example, certain of the so-called *simple cells* have a receptive field quite like that of the retinal ganglion cell except that the excitatory region of the field is elongated, and the inhibitory area surrounds and is parallel to it. Maximum response on the part of such a cell is obtained if a dark line on a bright background is aligned with the receptive field. Not unreasonably this kind of cell is known as a *line detector* (see also Ch. 7).

In addition, representing to some extent an increasing degree of particularity, there are *complex* and *hypercomplex* cells. Of these the complex cells are of interest in relation to the work on similarity grouping, since they are orientation-specific. The fact that orientation information is extracted so early in the visual processing sequence seems to be in agreement with the discussion of grouping.

Visual deprivation and learning to perceive

Early investigations of the effects on perception of being reared in the dark showed that subsequent visual behaviour was impaired relative to that of normally reared animals. But total isolation from light was found to result in irreversible damage to the retina. Later work showed that if the animals were reared in diffuse lighting conditions (perhaps by wearing a translucent hood) giving no opportunity for pattern vision, then various visually dependent skills like form discrimination were affected. The skills would often develop but not to a normal level. The evidence of recovery to any degree is itself of interest since it seems to show perceptual learning.

Some recent research has tried to discover how early the receptive field organization of adulthood is in evidence, and whether it is affected by early visual experience. If kittens are reared with a visual environment of stripes of a single orientation then the majority of visual cortical cells become responsive only to that orientation, very few being sensitive to orientation at right angles to it. Visual irregularities can be produced by short periods of the critical 'deprivation' experience just a few days after the animals' eyes normally open.

There is a long classical tradition of psychological studies on the problem of perceptual learning and there are many facets and qualifications that cannot be discussed here. Studies have been made of patients recovering from operations to remove cataracts that have made them blind since birth. The gradual emergence of visual skills in these individuals suggests that perceptual learning occurs. But such cases are hard to interpret since it is not clear to what extent they continue to rely on familiar sense modalities like touch and hearing.

The importance to normal perceptual development of coordinated opportunity for active movement was suggested by an experiment by Held and Hein (1963) in which kittens were reared in darkness except for occasional exposure (three hours a day) to the experimental condition. An apparatus was used with two kittens placed in baskets at opposite ends of a supporting arm which could rotate about its centre. One kitten was free to move around the circle, but the other was enclosed. However, as the free kitten moved so the restrained animal went around with him. Despite comparable visual experience only the active kitten developed perceptually while the passive one was effectively blind.

To discover how malleable is the adult perceptual system various individuals have worn, or have persuaded others to wear, spectacles that produced visual distortions. Stratton in the 1890s went about wearing a device that turned the retinal image so the top of an object was imaged where the bottom had been previously, and the left-hand and right-hand sides were also exchanged. As a result the retinal information about an object was directly at odds with the information fed back from the arm if it were to be correctly pointing at the object. Initially Stratton did indeed make the wrong movements when reaching out for things and became acutely disoriented in general. His perception of his own body was also distorted and not surprisingly the world looked upside-down.

After a few days Stratton gained more control over his body and could carry out simple tasks. His body image became more settled and the visual world about him appeared to be the right way up. Nevertheless disturbances of body image and vision continued and he would sometimes experience himself as upside-down although the world looked normal. Similar effects have been reported in other studies. Wearers of the distorting spectacles, who have incidentally undertaken alarmingly ambitious tasks like driving a car and skiing, give descriptions that suggest their perceptions were curiously disjointed and unstable.

Other experiments have resorted to less dramatic ways of producing perceptual rearrangements. Held and Bossom (1961) found that observers wearing prisms for a short period compensated for the distortion produced only if they were free to move about; individuals moved about in a wheelchair showed no sign of adapting. In general the evidence suggests that active movement is essential to perceptual adaptation.

We have taken the opportunity to introduce substantive psychological issues while taking a brief tour of inspection of the visual system. The psychological enquiries have been presented as side-shoots in the course of these introductory chapters. They do have considerable substance in their own right, of course. The question of physiological structure (but hopefully not the moral) will be largely set to one side in subsequent chapters. Measurement in perception is the focus of the next chapter; although related issues have already forced themselves on us from time to time they have generally been skirted, and it is now necessary to give them closer attention.

3
Weights and measures

It will by now be apparent that when we talk about a person's sensitivity in this book we do not mean his interpersonal skills, his ability to pick up 'bad vibes' or whatever (see B2). The problems we deal with here are more akin to a different set of everyday experiences in which our sense organs play a dominant role.

We are continually detecting, discriminating and judging on the basis of sensory data – noticing the smell of honeysuckle, testing whether there is sugar in the tea or salt in the potatoes, telling whether there is lipstick on someone's collar, responding to the telltale smell of a burning cigarette on the bedclothes, matching two shades of paint, deciding whether there was a knock at the door (or was it a mouse behind the skirting?), knowing when to put more hot water in the bath, assessing by the sound of a car whether it is approaching or receding, appreciating whether the light has faded too much for play to continue, judging the speed of oncoming traffic, deciding which is the heavier suitcase and so on. These manifestations of 'sensitivity' are no doubt less subtle than the interpersonal kind, but it is not always appreciated that they pose problems for the psychologist. The first is simply to specify a given situation in physical terms. Some situations are so complex that they are frankly intractable in this sense or involve so many variables that it may be necessary to abstract one aspect for study. So it may be more profitable to investigate sensitivity to simple lights, tones, odours etc. The problems of producing and controlling simple stimuli for experimental purposes may be considerable (as in experiments on taste and odour detection) but they are more approachable than the natural situations in the above examples.

Another issue concerns the nature of the task that we wish to investigate. We could seek to map out the range of responsiveness for a given sense modality (the spectacular sensitivity of the visual system will be remembered from Chapter 1). One set of questions about simplified situations follows:

How intense does a sound need to be before it can be heard? What is the least pressure applied to the skin that can be detected? By how much does the body have to be tilted out of the vertical for it to be noticeable? What is the least acceleration of the body that can be felt? What is the weakest solution of a substance (say, sugar) that can be tasted? What is the least smell (say, of mothballs) that can be detected?

All these 'refined' tasks put questions about *detection* and can be related to the absolute threshold task described in Chapter 1. This brings us up against another problem encountered there, the matter of choosing a *measurement procedure*. The last two questions are about taste and odour detection and their wording reinforces the importance of specifying the stimulus. In practice this turns out to be essential since, for example, the threshold for musk (in terms of the concentration of the substance in air) is much lower than for ether. This point was also made in Chapter 1 where we saw that the absolute threshold for vision depends on stimulus parameters like wavelength and area.

But we are not just concerned with the absolute limits of sensitivity and it is at least as important to know how sensation varies throughout the range of responsiveness. This almost begs the question of whether the measurement of sensation can be managed. *Can* we judge brightness or loudness? Nobody would dispute that the loudness of the output of a rock band or a pneumatic drill is greater than the rustling of leaves! It shows that we can make some simple ordering of levels of auditory stimulation. One question that follows from this is how small a difference it takes to make a difference. Another concerns whether a person can estimate, not just compare, levels of stimulation. Can he, for example, estimate loudness? If we can persuade him somehow to give a subjective measure of the magnitude of his sensation, then an interesting question will be how this subjective variable is related to a physical specification of the stimulus. It turns out that people do quite astonishingly well at metering sensations; so well in fact that the collection of methods developed to look at the problem has been exported to research areas where there is often no prospect of supplying a physical description of the stimulus (e.g. attitudes, preferences etc.) (see B3).

Psychophysical methods

Detection

The measurement of the threshold for light in Chapter 1 was an instance of a general class of measurement procedures used for estimating relations between psychological and physical variables called psychophysical methods. Methods for estimating detection thresholds inevitably involve the use of a range

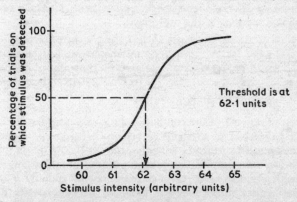

Fig. 3.1 *Schematic psychometric function for detection experiment*

of stimuli which are chosen to extend both above and below the threshold value. The main difference between the methods concerns the way in which the different stimulus values are presented to the observer. In the *method of limits* (p. 13) the values are presented in an orderly fashion, several times over, either ascending or descending through the series of values each time. In the dark adaptation experiment we used the ascending method of limits. Both ascending and descending series are used whenever practical, generally alternately, and the overall mean they produce is taken as the threshold.

If the *method of constant stimuli* is followed then the stimuli are presented in a random order. This is repeated several times so that for each intensity the proportion of trials can be found on which the stimulus was detected. In practice the proportion of detection responses increases as the intensity increases, as shown in Figure 3.1; this S-shaped curve is known as a *psychometric function*. The convention is to take the stimulus value giving rise to a detection rate of 50 per cent as the absolute threshold.

Discrimination

Some of the original instances of 'sensitivity' at the beginning of the chapter involved making comparisons, matching things, or discriminating between them. Therefore in principle we can distinguish detection tasks from those in which the job is to make a discrimination between two stimuli. Consider some 'refined' versions of the problem:

> By how much does the intensity of a light have to be increased (or decreased) before the change is reportable? How small a difference in the length of two lines can be discriminated? What is the smallest noticeable difference in the pitch of two tones?

So we are led to the concept of the *difference threshold*. A nice old-fashioned alternative label which has the great merit of being self-explanatory is the *just noticeable difference* (jnd) between two stimuli. In practice when the values of the stimuli are moved so close that the subject can no longer reliably discriminate between them, the margin between their values is taken as his difference threshold.

The distinction between detection and discrimination tasks is somewhat blurred by the presence of spontaneous neural activity in the nervous system which acts like a permanent background of 'noise' against which external stimuli have to be assessed. In effect even the detection task becomes one of discriminating between a signal embedded in 'noise' and the 'noise' only. Of course the experimenter will try to reduce unwanted external stimulation as much as possible, but the practicalities of doing this, in conjunction with the problem of irreducible neural noise, have led some investigators to impose noise signals of a kind that they can themselves control.

The psychophysical methods described for the detection task can be fairly directly adapted for the estimation of difference thresholds. A standard stimulus value is chosen together with a series of *comparison* or *variable* stimulus values ranging about the standard. A trial consists of presenting one comparison and the standard stimulus; the observer has to judge which of the two has more of the stimulus attribute in question. To obtain the difference threshold for line length the standard line is presented along with one of the comparison lines and the observer indicates which is the larger.

The observer may be given a simple 'larger'–'smaller' judgement or he may be allowed to use an 'equal' response category as well. The former two-choice procedure is briefly described below for the case of the *method of constant stimuli*. This is a generalization of the earlier constants method for detection thresholds and entails presenting the comparison values in a random order several times. On each trial the observer indicates which is the 'greater' (louder, larger, brighter, etc.) stimulus, and the proportion of occasions for a given comparison stimulus is found on which it was judged to be 'greater' than the standard. These proportions are plotted, as a psychometric function, against the values of the comparison stimuli (Fig. 3.2). It can be seen that as the value of the comparison stimulus increases so the probability of judging it to be greater than the standard increases.

Reading across from the 50 per cent point on the response axis the value can be found where the comparison is judged equal in value to the standard (follow the middle dotted line); this is known as the *point of subjective equality* (PSE). Two estimates of the jnd can be found. We take the comparison values corresponding to 25 and 75 per cent 'greater' judgements: they can be thought of respectively as the values when the comparison stimulus is judged just-noticeably-less and just-noticeably-greater than the standard. These two values span two jnds and the difference threshold is therefore taken as half their difference.

A relation between the jnd and the value of the standard has been demonstrated for certain continua. Provided the standard value is of moderate intensity the jnd tends to increase as the standard value increases, or put another way, the jnd is a constant proportion of the standard. This is called *Weber's Law* after the nineteenth-century physiologist who first reported it. It is supported by everyday experience: a candle lit in a dark room has a much greater effect on brightness than if it is placed in an already well-lit room; the conversational whisper in a library is more noticeable than the

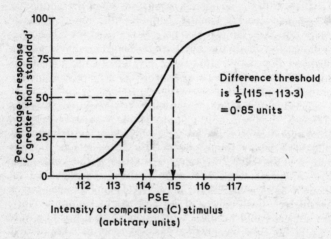

Fig. 3.2 *Schematic psychometric function for discrimination experiment*

question shouted against traffic noise; a spoonful of chilli pepper on an unseasoned dish is more obvious than an equal amount added to a hot curry.

Typical values of the Weber constant or fraction include 1/50 for lifted weight, 1/60 for brightness and 1/5 for the taste of a salt solution. Thus a 6 gm weight added to a weight of 300 gm will be just noticeable, as will be an additional 15 gm on top of 750. In these examples brightness is the sharpest, and taste the dullest, sense.

The Weber fraction for brightness discrimination follows an interesting course as the standard intensity varies. It decreases from a high value of 3 at very low intensities to about 1/60 at high intensities, with the now familiar evidence of a transition from rod to cone vision at intermediate intensities.

This aside, the tendency for the fraction to fall throughout the largest part of the range indicates that Weber's Law does not readily apply in this case.

Recognition and identification

The threshold methods can be adapted for use when there are a number of stimulus alternatives. For instance, we could measure the shortest amount of time required for some object to be identified. Duration thresholds of this kind have been recorded for graphic material – single letters, strings of letters, words, shapes, pictures etc. Commonly used for this purpose is the *tachistoscope* (see A9), a device which literally gives the observer the merest glimpse, of controlled duration, of the stimulus. An alternative is to increase the level of illumination until the stimulus can be correctly made out.

The task may require the subject to identify the stimulus although the term 'recognition' is used quite commonly. Recognition is reserved by some authorities to describe the situation where a limited set of alternatives is specified and known to the subject. However, identification and recognition tend to merge when it is realized that the former can be thought of as recognition from a large implicit collection of alternatives. For example, if the task was to identify a word, the subject could be considered to be recognizing it as one item of his own vocabulary. The task used by Menzer and Thurmond (1970) described in Chapter 2 is a mixture of detection (deciding whether a shape was presented) and recognition (deciding which of two alternatives it was). Previous research in that area had used identification tasks – where the subject had to produce the name of the object.

We have already noted the importance in the detection threshold procedure of ensuring that the observer maintains a stable criterion on which to base his response. If his willingness to make the response varies in the course of the experiment, then the effects of the variable under investigation may be obscured by or even mistaken for the shift in his response criterion. The problem is illustrated by the phenomenon of *perceptual defence*.

Consider the following hypothetical experiment. Using one of the standard psychophysical methods, thresholds are recorded for a collection of English words, including 'dirty' words like 'shit'. The experimenter finds that the dirty words have higher thresholds than 'neutral' words, i.e. they need a longer exposure duration to be recognized. It is tempting to conclude from this that the emotional properties of the dirty words have influenced the recognition process.

A critical colleague might point out that the dirty words were also different from the neutral words, for example, in terms of their word shapes. Our assiduous experimenter in reply might repeat the study including carefully chosen shape-mates of the dirty words in the pool of neutral ones (e.g. pairing shot with shit), and yet the difference between them is likely to persist.

Another sceptic could draw attention to the surprise or even plain embarrassment that some subjects experience at the prospect of voicing one of these dirty words in the company of the experimenter. Such subjects might suppress the 'dirty' responses at least long enough for the effect to show up in the form of heightened thresholds. The emphasis here is on the response aspects of the task. A somewhat subtler version of the criticism is that the dirty stimulus word arouses conflict and this inhibits the production of the response to it; this attributes the effect to processes of which the observer may be unaware but still emphasizes that the effect is on responding rather than perceiving.

A variety of ingenious methods have been used to circumvent the response problem in this particular case and they are discussed by Dixon (1971). For present purposes the important methodological question that emerges from this is whether we can devise ways of estimating the sensitivity of the observer uncontaminated by the criterion on which his response is based. A solution is discussed in the next section which has had a radical influence on psychophysical method and theory in general.

Signal detection theory

An unscrupulous or careless observer could seriously mislead the experimenter in the detection task by stating that he could detect the stimulus when he could not or by responding haphazardly some or all of the time. The experimenter, after all, has no direct way of checking the veracity of the responses he collects: they are the mirror of the observer's experiences and the experimenter's hope is that the mirror is not distorted. One check that has been employed is to include 'catch trials' in the procedure. These are trials on which, unknown to the subject, no stimulus is presented. It is assumed that if he responds on such a trial then he is guessing. Furthermore, the assumption is that this tendency to guess also applies on those occasions when the stimulus is not detected. By guessing on these trials too the subject will sometimes be right even though he misses the stimulus. The catch trials reflect the same predisposition to guess and the rationale for including them is therefore that they supply a basis for adjusting the observed detection rate.

An alternative approach insists that no distinction need be made between mechanisms for different responses since they are mediated by a common decision process. The argument is that on a given trial sensory evidence is accumulated and the response depends on whether this evidence meets a criterion set by the observer. This criterion is in the nature of a response threshold rather than a sensitivity limit. The point is made that the random neural noise in the system may reach a level which is judged, quite genuinely and not by guesswork, to arise from a signal externally. These are the beginnings of *signal detection theory* (Green and Swets, 1966).

Signal detection theory (SDT) is a theory about how evidence is treated in order to reach a decision. In principle, practically any decisions may be subjected to this kind of analysis. An essential feature is the concept of a decision axis or dimension any one value of which can exist at a given instant. From time to time the momentary value of this axis fluctuates (partly in response to variation in the residual noise in the system); in general, however, the existence of evidence for the decision (i.e. the signal is presented) leads to higher values than obtain in its absence. The stronger the evidence, the higher the average value achieved. The average increase in value induced by evidence of a constant strength is conventionally denoted by d'. This strength may be affected by many factors including the intensity of a sensory stimulus relative to background 'noise' and the efficiency of the sensory mechanisms involved. All else being equal, d' is taken as an index of the sensitivity of the subject.

The problem remains for the decision process of fixing the regions on the decision axis to be associated with the available response alternatives. So each of the responses has to be associated with or 'mapped' onto a particular region of decision axis values. Frequently the subject is allowed only two responses, such as deciding that something is or is not there. This mapping problem is overcome, in the theory at any rate, by selecting a point on the decision axis and operating a decision rule which links the response 'Yes' to values on the decision axis greater than the cut-off point, and the response 'No' to lower values. The position of this cut-off point is defined numerically and is by convention called β. The position of the cut-off point, or criterion, is not arbitrary. It may be shown mathematically that there is an optimal value of β depending upon the relative frequency of occurrence of the event in question and the pay-offs (rewards and punishments) associated with detecting and not detecting it when it is or is not present. Thus, for example, if the event is rare and the profit for a correct detection is small compared with the loss associated with crying 'wolf' (a false positive response), it will be optimal to set the criterion to a high value. This will minimize the chances of reporting the signal even when it is absent while still correctly detecting it most (but not all) of the time it is actually present. While it is possible to state what the 'ideal observer' would do in terms of choosing a value of β, it is valuable to calculate after the event what value was actually chosen because this gives a measure of the response bias adopted by the subject. A low value of β implies a bias towards responding 'Yes', and a high value means bias against.

The significance of SDT is two-fold. First it challenges the traditional idea of the threshold as an inviolable boundary to sensation. In fact, it asserts that there is no need for the concept of a *sensory* threshold, and focuses attention instead on the psychophysical task as a decision-making affair in which the subject's main job is to establish a criterion for responding in the face of continuously varying sensory evidence. By this shift of emphasis it has pointed to the importance of non-sensory situational factors likely to affect the setting of the response criterion (and hence the apparent sensory limitations of the subject).

The evidence suggests that indeed non-sensory variables are important, and that subjects tend to respond to changes in the relative frequency of occurrence of signals, and changes in the pay-offs. Moreover, although they tend to be somewhat conservative about the extent to which they are prepared to switch criterion values, they nevertheless do so in a direction that the ideal observer would do. For example, if the relative frequency of a signal is high then a low criterion (corresponding to less evidence) should be and indeed is adopted.

The second thrust of SDT is methodological. It represents an important contribution to the repertoire of measurement techniques available to perception and indeed general psychology. It has been applied, without prejudice to psychophysical theory, in a variety of circumstances where the task for the subject can be construed as one involving decision-making in the face of uncertain evidence (see Ch. 6). It promises a way of estimating the separate contributions of sensory and response factors.

For example, SDT offers a way of tackling, if not resolving, the dispute about perceptual defence. Hardy and Legge (1968) applied SDT in an experiment where the subject was asked to detect faint tones while looking at an apparently blank screen. In fact the screen was occasionally faintly illuminated by emotive words like 'cancer'. The results suggested that there was a reduction in sensitivity on the detection task (i.e. d' decreased) whenever an emotional stimulus provided the subliminal accompaniment. There were other complications, however, suggesting that the response criterion β was also affected in a rather involved fashion.

An intriguing application of SDT was reported by Clark and Goodman (1974) who set out to investigate the effect of instruction on the detection of pain. Heat stimuli were used for the purpose and subjects had to say when pain was detected. One set of instructions was designed to get the subject to respond to the least amount of pain, and another to indicate only when he was certain that the stimulus was painful (different groups of subjects were used). The pain 'threshold' varied along with this change in instructions as might by now be expected. But the change was due to a difference in the response criteria adopted (lower when minimal pain was to be reported), while d' was unaffected. Interestingly men set higher criteria than women, although their sensitivity to pain did not differ.

Despite the obsessive interest shown by psychophysics about responsiveness to marginal stimuli, we should remember that the bulk of our existence is spent responding to levels of stimulation that are far from marginal, and may be noticeably graduated. We are most likely to become aware of them when they change, as when a cold draught of air is produced by opening a window, when a cloud passes over the sun, or when the radio is turned up suddenly.

In fact psychophysics is just as concerned with the relation between the psychological variable and its physical counterpart throughout the full range of physical magnitudes. To specify this relation is to specify a psychological scale. To ask why the relation takes the particular form it does is to ask a question about the 'psychophysical law'.

In the mid-nineteenth century Fechner described how the jnd could be used to form a scale of sensation magnitude and went on to formulate his version of the psychophysical law. He made two assumptions, first that Weber's Law was correct (see p. 42), and second that jnds are *subjectively* equal throughout the range of stimulus intensities. Thus a single jnd can be used as the unit of subjective or sensation magnitude. From Weber's Law we know that the physical value of the jnd increases as the standard intensity increases. But the subjective value of a jnd is constant. Putting these two assumptions together it follows that increases in sensation magnitude will correspond to larger and larger increases in physical magnitude (see Fig. 3.3).

Fechner reasoned further that this relation between the psychological and physical scales was logarithmic. Data in the form of Figure 3.3 would tend to support this, although it would be more convenient to have a logarithmic scale on the horizontal axis to reflect the nature of this version of the psychophysical law. The logarithmic law was put to the test with another scaling method called *category scaling*. In this task each of the stimuli have to be assigned to one of a specified number of categories. The observer is instructed to use the scale so that the difference in the subjective magnitudes between two adjacent categories is the same at all points on the scale; this is the defining characteristic of an interval scale (see

A8). Typically an odd number of categories is used, say five, seven or nine.

The evidence from category scale studies for the logarithmic law is mixed. *Prothetic* continua – those where stimulus values are additive like brightness, loudness or heaviness – give positive support; the relation between the category scale

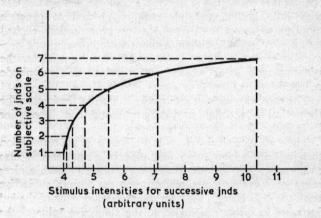

Fig. 3.3 *Growth of sensation on a jnd scale*

values and the physical scale is as expected. But the logarithmic relation is not obtained with the *metathetic* continua – where stimulus values are substituted for one another – like pitch, apparent location or hue.

A collection of methods, developed by S. S. Stevens, are thought to lead to ratio scales (where not only differences but also ratios between values are meaningful; see A8) and represent something of a breakthrough in psychological scaling. These methods have a disarming simplicity. The following quotation from Stevens (1971) gives typical instructions for a subject in a magnitude estimation experiment; the italicized words have been added to make the example more specific:

You will be presented with a series of stimuli in irregular order. Your task is to tell how *bright* they seem by assigning numbers to them. Call the first stimulus any number that seems to you appropriate. Then assign successive numbers in such a way that they reflect your subjective impression. For example, if a stimulus seems 20 times as *bright*, assign a number 20 times as large as the first. If it seems one-fifth as *bright*, assign a number one-fifth as large, and so forth. Use fractions, whole numbers, or decimals, but make each assignment proportional to the *brightness* as you perceive it.

Given all the cautions which have hedged us about in this chapter it is reassuring to find that people do this kind of task with little hesitation: they happily proceed to generate numbers to reflect the magnitudes of the sensations elicited by different stimuli. Other methods include *magnitude production*, where a number is given and the subject adjusts the stimulus to a value which gives the sensation magnitude reflected by the number.

The ease with which these methods are practised belies the theoretical thicket that has sprung up round them. The major issue is the psychophysical law again.

There is no particular merit in Fechner's second assumption that jnds are subjectively equal, especially since there seems to be no satisfactory way of testing it directly. With a nicer sense of symmetry one might come up with a subjective analogue of Weber's Law, that the subjective value of the jnd increases in direct proportion to the subjective value of the standard. It was this essential difference in assumptions that led Stevens to reformulate the psychophysical law – sensation magnitude is a power function of the physical magnitude, i.e. sensation magnitude varies according to the physical value raised to a power. This is Stevens' *power law*.

The power law can be tested by plotting both sensation and physical magnitudes on logarithmic scales. Should a straight line result then the power law is supported. The slope of the straight line is an important quantity since this represents the exponent (n) or power of the power function. According to *sensory transducer theory* (Stevens, 1961) the exponent reflects the nature of the neural mechanisms involved in converting or transducing the stimulus energy into a neural code. The exponent for brightness has been estimated at 0·33 and that for electric shock applied through the fingertips is about 3·5. Figure 3.4 shows how the brightness and shock sensations grow as stimulus intensity increases. The exponent for light may reflect the 'compression' achieved by the sensory transducers to deal with the vast range of intensities to which they are sensitive. Conversely the sensory transducers for shock

50

have a high exponent, indicating an 'expansion' effect which seems to have biological value in the face of potentially damaging stimulation like electric current.

The power law has been found to apply for over thirty continua that have been investigated. These include loudness, brightness, smell (e.g. coffee), taste (e.g. sucrose, salt), temperature, vibration, pressure on palm, heaviness, muscle tension and shock. Low and moderate temperatures of course give rise to sensations we describe as cold and warm; interestingly they have different exponents, and Stevens concluded

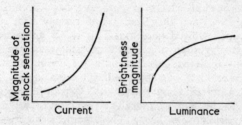

Fig. 3.4 *Growth of sensation magnitude for electric shock and brightness (schematic)*

that this may signify a transducer difference. Muscle tension is produced by asking the subject to squeeze the handle of a dynamometer, a device which enables the force applied to be measured; the magnitude of the sensation so produced varies with the force, and according to the power law.

The relation between experiences in different modalities has been investigated by the method of *cross-modality matching*. Essentially the observer is asked to adjust the value of a stimulus in one modality until the sensation magnitude it produces is equal to that produced by a second stimulus in a second modality. Thus he may be asked to adjust a light until it is as bright as a tone is loud. Comparisons of this sort have been made for loudness and vibration, shock and force of handgrip, and many more. Since sound engineers refer to 'bright sounds', poets describe sensations of one kind in the terms of another, and we habitually use descriptions like 'a thunderous glare', it is not surprising that we can manage these kinds of task.

By assuming that the power law applies to each of two

continua, it can be shown that the objective magnitudes of two stimuli that produce equal sensations should be in a fixed proportion to one another. Furthermore, this fixed proportion is predictable from the exponents for the two continua. This has been confirmed experimentally for several modalities and represents strong support for the power law (Stevens, 1961).

The amount of data supporting the power law is by now quite overwhelming. Nevertheless judgement can be reserved for a number of reasons. Although the exponent ought not to depend on the stimuli used, its size in scaling tasks shows a marked tendency to decrease as the range of stimuli values increases. Several effects of this sort have been reported (Poulton, 1968) and they lead one to suppose that response bias may be involved here too. This is not an entirely unreasonable suggestion since there may indeed be peculiarities about the way individuals use and appreciate numbers.

The power law can be predicted from quite different premises as described by Warren (1973), who proposed an alternative to the sensory transducer hypothesis. Warren calls this *physical correlate theory*. The argument is that estimates of sensory magnitudes are based on estimates of physical magnitudes, as opposed to being given as the result of some quite direct neural transformation.

Loudness and brightness, for example, are judged by estimating the change in stimulation otherwise associated with a change in distance. Some elegant experiments have been done in support of this theory. In one study the subject was asked to adjust the intensity of a variable light to a level corresponding to half that of a fixed standard light. He was in addition instructed to adjust the light so that it had the appearance of a light twice as far away. The results of the two methods agreed. Furthermore the half-brightness estimates were less accurate if the distance of the lights was harder to judge. Another neat demonstration of these effects was that the subject could accurately attenuate the loudness of a self-generated sound when asked to keep constant the intensity of this sound at a distant microphone; thus if the distance between himself and the microphone was doubled, he halved the pressure of the sound he produced. On the other hand, although these findings suggest how sensation may be estimated in certain circumstances, they do not seem to contradict Stevens' theory.

Whatever the fate of the power law, scaling methods are here to stay. Besides being applied to situations where a psychological variable has an obvious, specifiable, physical counterpart as in the examples above, they may also be used where the stimulus property is itself not known or measurable (as in the experiment by Beck on page 27 where a magnitude estimate of the degree of segregation of stimulus elements was used). Thus they can be used 'to gauge the consensus concerning intensity or degree for such variables as strength of expressed attitudes, pleasantness of musical selections, seriousness of crimes, and other subjective dimensions ...' (Stevens, 1966, p. 530). This and related techniques represent a significant enlargement of psychology's methodological basement.

4
Information acquisition

Perception is about the extraction of information from the external environment. It involves the operation of the senses and is effected in the shadow of the expectations, hopes, fears, needs and memories that make up our internal world. Monitoring, noticing, looking, watching, listening, observing, searching, examining, viewing, spectating, inspecting – these are some of the terms we use to describe activities that are of interest in the next three chapters. The essence of the problem is how we locate or acquire information.

They are activities which involve the deployment of our sensory or receptive systems, the direction and redirection of attention. They may be obviously purposive, active and selective, and the achievement may be unsubtle – as when we look up the meaning of a word in a dictionary, or search for a number in a telephone directory, or turn to discover who called our name. But the nature of the behaviour may be much less transparent and it may not be at all clear whether it is useful or appropriate to describe it in terms of purpose, activity and selection. Consider, for example, the activity of the spectator in an art gallery or at a football match, the listener to Radio 1, or a television viewer.

Despite some understandable reluctance to tangle with situations that inevitably involve many variables, there are a number of important investigations of looking and listening. But there are some notable differences in the styles of these two research areas which perhaps reflect fundamental differences between the visual and auditory systems. Experiments on listening have been primarily concerned with how limited resources for receiving information are allocated when there is more than a single task to be performed at a time. Thus the focus of interest has been mainly on the selection of information. This problem is discussed in Chapter 6.

Research on looking and searching has generally used one task at a time and the emphasis has been on what the observer looks at, what speeds him up and slows him down, and so on. Although there may be a speed emphasis, and some selectivity of information is implied, the interest is not in whether he can do two things at once but in how he achieves one thing at a time.

The great attraction of the visual system for attention research is that it is possible with suitable apparatus to discover what a person is looking at and where he moves his eyes to. The assumption can be made that what he looks at is what he attends to. Although this plausible assumption is questioned later, eye movement research has provided us with an important source of evidence about visual attention and visual behaviour in general. The importance of eye movements as an indicator of internal states 'was appreciated very well by oriental merchants, poets and policemen at least as long ago as it was by psychologists' (Alpern, 1971, p. 369).

Eye movements

As we saw in Chapter 1 the fovea of the retina is a region of high acuity extending over a visual angle of about 2 degrees. Eye movements, with supplementary assistance from head and body movements, enable us to make use of this high acuity property over the entire visual environment. The eyes can be moved by means of the ocular muscles (see Fig. 1.2) which are attached at points which enable the eye to make vertical, horizontal and, to a small extent, rotational (rolling) movements.

There are two main classes of eye movements, those that involve the movement of the eyes so that the angle between the two lines of sight is constant and those when the angle changes. The latter are used when the eyes fixate on an object moving towards them. The former may be subdivided into *saccadic eye movements* or saccades, sudden rapid shifts in fixation used in scanning a stationary object, and *pursuit eye movements* which are comparatively smooth, slow, tracking movements of the eyes used in visually following a moving object. We shall not deal with the latter.

On the occasions when the eye is steadily fixated on an object, i.e. between large-scale saccades, one has the impression that there is no movement at all, but in practice there is an accompaniment of miniature eye movements. There are very small saccades, one to three times a second and involving a movement of about six minutes of arc (equivalent to the size of a 2p coin at about 150 cm), slow drifting movements, and a continual very rapid tremor. The miniature saccades have usually been interpreted as having a corrective function; however, it has recently been suggested that they accomplish nothing (Steinman, Haddad, Skavenski and Wyman, 1973)! The tremor component consists of a high frequency oscillation of the eye (with roughly one-twentieth of the amplitude of miniature saccades). It is called physiological nystagmus and, unlike the miniature saccades, it is indisputably important in the maintenance of vision.

The effect of nystagmus is to continually shift the image on the retina; however, by means of a physical linkage between the eye and the object being inspected it can be arranged for the retinal image to be stationary. One method is to attach the 'target' to be inspected to a contact lens arrangement worn by the observer. In this way the image is projected onto the same retinal cells; the outcome is a *stabilized retinal image*. As a result, intriguing changes take place in the appearance of the object. Its hue and form are affected, with a fading of the former and a disappearance of components of the latter. Fragmentation of forms was described by Pritchard (1961): when the word BEER was stabilized the observers reported seeing the fragments PEER, BEE, BEEP and BE etc. The nature of the disappearance is of interest since it seemed to be quite systematic as meaningful units of the stimuli tended to disappear; but it is easy to see that response bias and the difficulty of reporting random or partial fragmentation might exaggerate this effect.

The effects can also be produced by viewing in poor lighting conditions or using blurred targets. It seems that the receptors cease to respond if a steady image is projected onto them and physiological nystagmus has the effect of continually calling fresh receptors into service.

Nevertheless, despite physiological nystagmus and the tiny intermittent adjustments to the visual apparatus, perception is more or less continuous during fixations. Indeed visual perception is essentially continuous despite large-scale eye movements too. This in itself is a remarkable and little understood achievement, particularly in view of the intermittent loss of visual sensitivity during eye movements described below.

Measurement of eye movements is made by all manner of devices which allow various aspects of visual behaviour to be specified. Of interest is the time span of fixations and saccades, and the distance travelled between successive fixations. Above all, of course, the investigator may want to have data about where in the visual field, on what objects, the observer fixated.

One method capitalizes on the fact that there are systematic changes in the electrical potential that can be recorded from the skin around the eyes and which are a direct reflection of the direction of the eye movement. By placing electrodes above and below the eye these potential changes can be converted into a record of horizontal and vertical motion of the eyes. Photographic methods have also been used. One of the techniques involves projecting a small light onto the cornea, the reflection of which moves as the eye does. It can be arranged for this light spot to be photographed in such a way that it is superimposed on the visual scene in front of the observer; as a result the successive frames of the film indicate the position of the eye relative to the scene.

Application of these methods has revealed a wealth of information about the nature of large-scale or *major* eye movements. At the more quantitative level, saccades take about 150 to 200 thousandths of a second (milliseconds or ms) to initiate and a further 30 to 90 ms to complete (Bartz, 1962), although these durations vary somewhat with the angular distance moved. Other studies have reported rather longer latencies, in the range 250–280 ms. It has been suggested that the voluntary saccade is ballistic, that is, it cannot be corrected or cancelled once begun (cf. Ch. 4 in A5).

Westheimer (1954) instructed his subjects to look at a spot of light which was then shifted. If it returned to the original position very quickly (within 50 ms) the saccade took place despite this, even though the spot had returned over 100 ms before the eye had even begun to move. This has been taken to support the view that data are accepted by the visual system on a discontinuous basis, and that in this case information about the location of the spot and the position of the eye is only collected about five times a second.

Vision is affected during eye movements. The extreme view that vision is lost is certainly not tenable, but sensitivity is impaired not only during the execution of a saccade but also for about 50 ms before it is initiated.

Studies of eye movements have tended to concentrate on the locus and duration of fixation. Average durations drawn from several sources vary between 250 and 350 ms. Fixation times may well vary with the kind of task but this has not been extensively investigated, although variations in the demands of a given task have been studied. Gould (1967) recorded fixation times from subjects carrying out a matching task in which they were required to check how many times a standard pattern occurred among a set of comparison patterns. Fixations lasted about 340 ms when the target and comparisons were highly similar but 280 ms in a low-similarity condition. In addition stimuli that matched the standard were fixated for rather longer than non-matching patterns. This suggests that fixation duration indicates the time taken to register and process the stimulus. On this reasoning fixation times in reading would be expected to be longer for harder material, since presumably it would require more processing. But Buswell (1922) found little variation in fixation times with the difficulty of reading material.

The fixation time is also spent making small initial saccadic adjustments. It seems likely that a decision is made during this interval about where to locate future fixations. One possibility is that the initial stage of a fixation is occupied by extracting information from the present fixation locus and the last part of the interval is devoted to acquiring information about the next (or maybe the next but one) place to fixate. Alternatively both operations could be carried out at once, or they could be interleaved (first a bit of one job, then a bit of the other, and so on). The plain fact is that there is little direct evidence that can be called on.

Location and pattern of fixations

Several studies have been concerned with the intriguing question of what people look at, and have recorded the position of the eyes as well as timing their movements. Gould and Schaffer (1965), using a number matching task, found that the most confusable digits (like 2, and 9) were fixated most closely. Using patterns like random bar charts, Gould and Dill (1969) found that fixations were most frequently aimed at targets if they and the non-targets were dissimilar, but if they were alike the two were fixated about equally often. This suggests that targets and non-targets may be discriminated via peripheral vision if similarity is low, but if they closely resemble one another the fovea is more likely to be needed.

Williams (1966) recorded eye movements while his subjects searched for a given number among about 100 others. Each number was printed inside a figure which could vary in colour, shape and size. Besides the target number the other incidental attributes of the figure could be specified. Thus the subject might have to look for the '32-green' or the '16-very small pink cross' or simply the '29', and so on. When the target was specified along with its colour (e.g. '31-red') there was a marked tendency for fixations to fall on figures of that colour. But there was little evidence of this when its shape was given and this was true also for the size attribute except for the 'very large' category. Combined information about two or all three attributes did not confer an extra advantage in terms of fixation rate.

Only colour consistently, and size to some extent, was useful in enabling the subject to structure the visual field perceptually. Targets were also located most rapidly when fixations indicated that the incidental information was being used. These findings suggest that in a crowded visual display extrafoveal guidance can be achieved quite effectively by colour, but not by shape. The success of the largest size category is consistent with the hypothesized summative property of extrafoveal vision (p. 23).

Yarbus (1967) recorded eye movements of people while they gazed at pictures. Fixations clustered in particular regions which depended on the instructions the subject was given. In general, features that were significant for the task were fixated. For example, fixations on a picture of some people in a room fell on the people when their ages had to be estimated, but when their material well-being had to be judged fixations were more dispersed and drawn more to the objects in the room. Moreover there seemed to be some cyclical scan of these important features.

Although we may receive the impression that we see a picture at a glance there is evidently more to it than this and a complicated sequence of eye movements is involved. And yet when we learn that these eye movements do occur and do so in an organized fashion then it makes intuitive sense that they fall on what we think of as significant features. Mackworth and Morandi (1967) asked one group of people to look at pictures and to judge what they found most 'informative'. Another group merely looked at the same pictures but their eye fixations were recorded. There was good agreement between what was considered informative and what was looked at most often. This is a clear demonstration, since different groups of subjects were used, so the results are not due to the same subjects interpreting different instructions in a common way as so often happens. The fixation pattern was very quickly established, essentially without scanning the entire display. It was concluded that areas were effectively designated as 'unwanted' via peripheral vision.

In reading the eyes follow the direction of the text, from left to right, and top to bottom of the page. Highly skilled readers or individuals just 'skimming' the text may need only one or two fixations per line, but more are needed if the material is technical or difficult. Occasionally regressive eye movements may be made when the reader backtracks to clarify something. Regressions are often thought to be more typical of the unskilled or beginning reader, but they are not all that more frequent in children (about 25 per cent) than in fluent adults (about 15 per cent). Fixations in reading may be located 'in any part of the words, or in the spacing between them' (Dearborn, 1906). However, Dearborn also reported that 'prepositional phrases and relative clauses ... require most fixations'. These and other findings suggest that fixations might be 'controlled' in part by phrase size. However, later evidence (e.g. Morton, 1964) supports the view that fixations do not fall in regions of particular syntactic, or semantic, significance. It seems that fixations in reading seem not to be drawn by any particular feature of the text. The eye in fact 'runs ahead' of the voice when reading aloud by a matter of four or five words. This can be seen by turning the light off when someone is reading (then duck!). The number of words he can read after the light goes out is taken as a measure of his *eye–voice span*. This tends to increase as the 'meaningfulness' of the text increases (Morton, 1964), although this is not always easy to interpret since the subject may be able to guess more of a meaningful passage.

Snyder (1973) reported an interesting piece of applied psychological research on air-to-ground search. The eye movements of five test-pilots were recorded as they looked for target objects in a film of a low-level flight over a test range. Fixation patterns were concentrated near the horizon and in the centre of the field, falling mainly on certain features like clearings and roads. Some 80–90 per cent of the fixations fell within 5 per cent of the visual scene.

An incidental finding reported by Snyder that bears on the interpretation of eye movement records is that his test-pilots would occasionally look at a target region without detecting the target. Evidently what a man looks at may not necessarily be what he notices. There is in addition some evidence that suggests that what a man looks at is not necessarily an accurate indicator of what he is attending to. The evidence is from a study by Kaufman and Richards (1969). In one phase of their experiment the subject was asked to indicate at random points in time what he was looking at while inspecting a figure, and in a second phase the locations on which he fixated were recorded. The method used to discover the fixation locations is of interest because it ultimately depended on a subjective report. The lens of the eye has a crystalline structure, called the Haidinger brush, which ordinarily is not visible but under suitable lighting conditions, using polarized light and a rotating polarizing filter, can be seen. When made visible by this procedure what is seen resembles a fuzzy whirling propellor projected on the scene being viewed, and it is not construed as having an internal origin.

In the second part of the experiment Kaufman and Richards caused the Haidinger brushes to become visible on a number of occasions while the subject was inspecting the figure, with the instruction for him to report the location of the 'propeller'. By this means the fixation location can be assessed without the need for the subject to wear possibly constraining apparatus. It was found that subjects reported looking at a widely distributed set of locations whereas their fixations tended to cluster around the centre of the figure. Although this suggests that attending and fixating may be rather different, this ingenious fixation recording method may also be intrusive and constraining although in a different sense to the usual methods. The demands of the two tasks, looking and 'brush-detecting', seem to be quite different, and the experiment would stand repeating with a different fixation recording method.

Scanpaths and recognition

Observers not only tend visually to visit and revisit particular regions of a picture they are viewing, but they also carry out this tour of inspection in a fairly regular order. Thus the fixation pattern is not only spatial but temporal. This supports and extends the earlier finding by Yarbus (1967) that fixations tended to occur in cyclical fashion. This research was conducted by Noton and Stark (1971) who described the spatio-temporal fixation sequence as a *scanpath*. The scanpath emerges in the course of initially viewing a figure and tends to recur on later occasions, occupying about 30 per cent of the viewing period. Scanpaths seem to be related to significant features of the figure (Fig. 4.1) but are otherwise idiosyncratic.

The same scanpaths were adopted on about 65 per cent of occasions in a later 'recognition' phase of the experiment, when the original five figures were presented for inspection in a random order that included five figures not seen previously. The subjects were asked merely to 'observe' the figures as before but subsequently reported no difficulty in recognizing the 'old' figures. Although the tendency to adopt a scanpath was marked at all stages of the experiment it is worth recording that it was not universal. Noton and Stark concluded that the memory representation of a figure consists of a network of features, together with a record of the shifts of attention needed to pass through the network from feature to feature. The dominant or preferred route through this network corresponds to the scanpath.

Scanpaths were also observed by Locher and Nodine (1974) whose subjects were directly instructed to memorize a series of random shapes while their eye movements were recorded. A methodological improvement in this study was that its

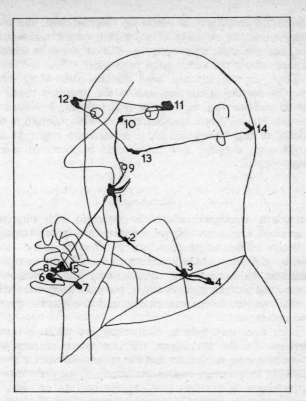

Fig. 4.1 *Scanpath of a subject viewing a drawing adapted from Paul Klee's 'Old man figuring' (from Noton and Stark, 1971: copyright © 1971 by Scientific American, Inc; all rights reserved)*

The order of the subject's fixations on the picture during part of a twenty-second viewing is shown by the numbers 1–14. Eye movements are shown by the lines connecting the fixations.

recognition phase was designed so that an explicit recognition response was obtained for each shape and the task was sufficiently hard for recognition to be less than perfect. This enabled recognition accuracy to be related to other factors, although in practice recognition accuracy was still rather too high to give much opportunity for variation between experimental conditions to show up. Nevertheless, the data suggest that the existence of a scanpath during memorizing does not guarantee subsequent recognition, nor does absence of scanpaths at the earlier stage preclude it.

These experiments use large displays, subtending more than 20 degrees at the eye, and so the 'attention shifts' of Noton and Stark's theory can be straightforwardly related to eye movements. Noton and Stark nevertheless referred to the possibility that these attentional adjustments might be internal ones, although how these could be identified is not clear.

Searching

Some eye movement research is concerned with what observers do when searching for predetermined targets among a collection of non-target items (e.g. the experiments by Gould and by Williams). Other visual search experiments have concentrated on performance characteristics like frequency of errors, and time to locate a target, generally using tasks with symbols (digits, letters, shapes, dials and so on) as the targets and non-targets.

Such data may help in discovering the subject's *search strategy*. On the assumption that the search strategy will affect how long it takes to find the target, one can go a surprisingly long way in making predictions about performance. Krendel and Wodinsky (1960) approached the problem by working out the nature of the distribution of search times to be expected on the basis of randomness. The subject's task was to locate a near-threshold spot of light on a large screen. The form of the distribution was as predicted and these experimenters concluded that successive 'glimpses' (i.e. fixations) taken in the course of searching were independent of one another. However, other research described in Howarth and Bloomfield (1971) suggests that searching may not be methodical but it is not generally random (many of us would no doubt vouch for the non-methodical character of our own efforts at finding missing shoes, etc.).

An alternative way of tackling the problem of the search strategy is to ask the observer what strategy he used! There is always a problem about doing this since it may be hard to describe the activity verbally. Furthermore, unless he is asked to make a special effort not to forget them he may not recall the details of where he looked, and if he is instructed to remember them then this may influence how he sets about the task and thus affect the strategy he uses. Dale (1964) found that subjects who adopted 'non-systematic' strategies tended to forget the region they searched. He also found that they did not always adopt the method they thought would be most efficient.

Attentional fields

How quickly visual information can be acquired depends on the position of the source of information in the visual field. Using a range of visual tasks, Sanders (1963) found that performance was related to visual angle but not in a simple linear way. Performance decreased as visual angle increased but showed particularly noticeable drops at two points. The first drop was at about 20 to 35 degrees into the periphery and the second somewhere between 75 and 105 degrees. This led Sanders to distinguish between three zones of the 'functional visual field': the first is called the *stationary field*, where performance requires no more than peripheral vision; the second is the *eye field*, a region where eye movements are required for the task to be carried out; and the third is known as the *head field*, which refers to the region where head movements are also needed.

In one task there were two columns of dots displayed simultaneously and the subject had to make one of four different responses depending on the patterns of dots the two columns contained. The ease of discriminating the patterns varied as well as the display angle between columns. A performance measure of response speed was used and this decreased with visual angle. Moreover the transitions from one field to another did not take place at fixed points but tended to depend on the difficulty of the task – the harder the task, the earlier the transition.

Within the stationary field the stimuli are handled in a single operation, but two intakes of information are needed in the head field. In the case of the eye field, information is again acquired in two chunks but the eye field enables valid hypotheses to be constructed in advance so that the processing of the second chunk is more efficient than the first

(Sanders, 1963). This implies that the extreme periphery supplies the wherewithal for the construction of the hypothesis about what the second signal is.

Other important research on the capabilities of the stationary field has extended the findings reported here and in Chapter 2. The discussion of these findings, suggesting for instance that even features of meaning can be picked up via extrafoveal vision, is continued in Chapter 9. We next consider some research in a rather different methodological tradition, concerned with the question of what can be seen in a single glance.

5
Perception in a glance

Many of the experiments in Chapter 4 gave full rein to the observer's visual system in the sense that eye and head movements were allowed, and in fact were often the focus of interest. In studies of the stationary field they have to be prevented either by request or by design. Some investigators have simply asked their subjects to keep their eyes still while looking at a display. Naturally this is not the easiest of tasks, but by taking the precaution of recording eye movements at the same time the experimenter can be sure of those occasions on which the instructions were followed. This was done by Menzer and Thurmond (see Ch. 2).

An alternative solution is to present the display, while the observer is fixating, for such a brief interval that the eyes are unlikely to move from the fixation point. The tachistoscope (p. 43), or a projector with a camera shutter attachment, can be used for this purpose. One of the many questions that have been tackled in this way is that of how much information can be acquired in a single glance.

The classical method of investigating this question was simply to expose briefly a display containing a number of items with the instruction to the subject to report as many as he could. The earliest findings pitched this limit somewhere between three and five when the display contained letters (Woodworth and Schlosberg, 1954). This limit on performance was referred to as the span of apprehension, and was considered to be perceptual in origin.

However, it has been pointed out that in fact the limiting factor in these experiments may not be perceptual. After all, goes the argument, the subject has to remember the items, so that his performance may be due to memory limitations. A long-standing complaint of people taking part in perceptual span studies is that their memory for the items displayed 'fades' before they have an opportunity of reporting all the items they saw clearly at the outset (Woodworth, 1938). The problem then is to measure the efficiency of the perceptual processes without relying too heavily on the resources of memory.

It was with this in mind that Sperling (1960) devised the *partial report* method. A display is used in which the items, perhaps letters of the alphabet, are organized in a square or rectangular formation. Thus, twelve letters could be presented as three rows with four letters in each row. The display is presented for a brief interval as usual, but immediately following it a 'cue' is presented as to which of the rows the subject is to report. Since he has no way of telling in advance which row is in question, it is assumed that the proportion of the cued row that he reports can serve to estimate the proportion of the entire display that was available to him. So, if he reports two out of a row of four items from a three-by-four display then it is assumed that six items were in fact available (two in each row).

Sperling found by this means that up to nine items were available from twelve-item displays when only four to five could be reported from the same material if the usual total report method was used. This effect has been replicated many times, although as we shall see its interpretation remains controversial. Sperling also studied the effect of varying the interval between the display and the cue (a high, medium or low tone denoted the row to be reported). He found that the span decreased as the interval increased, and that if the cue was withheld for one or two seconds then performance dropped to the level of a full report trial. This particular finding has been interpreted as showing the existence of a *sensory storage* system which can hold a great deal of information, but whose contents are rapidly lost unless they are transferred to a more permanent system or one in which they can be refreshed or rehearsed. The short-term storage system described by Gregg (see A6) is thought to be the most likely candidate as the next link in the processing sequence. A sensory store of this kind is considered to be an essential first component in most contemporary theories of visual processing. It was called the visual information store (VIS) by Sperling (1960), the sensory buffer by Atkinson and Shiffrin (1968) and, most graphically, the icon or iconic memory by Neisser (1967).

The VIS provides a way of extending the life of a stimulus. Evidence of visual persistence has been obtained by the disarmingly direct method of asking subjects to estimate the duration of a visual display. Thus Haber and Standing (1970) presented a flash of light and along with this a brief click. The display and click were repeated as a pair every few seconds and the subject had to adjust the apparatus producing the click until it appeared to coincide with the onset of the flash. This was done a second time but now the task was to synchronize the click with the offset of the flash. By taking the difference in the two time settings the effective duration of the flash could be estimated. Haber and Standing found that stimuli that lasted less than 100 ms were estimated as longer by about 200 ms, but if the stimulus was longer than about 300 ms or so there was no such persistence effect. Greater persistence was found if the subject was darkadapted, suggesting the effect is indeed visual.

Further evidence of visual persistence comes from an experiment by Eriksen and Collins (1967) in which two dot patterns were presented with a brief interval between them. The patterns were constructed so that when seen alone they looked like a random smattering of dots, but if superimposed they formed a short meaningless letter string. Provided the interval was 100 ms or less the two sets of dots could be merged or integrated into a single percept and the letters reported at a better-than-chance level. This seems to demonstrate the persistence of the first of the two stimuli. The quality of this representation evidently decreased as the interval increased, since performance fell systematically to reach a steady level at 300 ms where presumably persistence was no longer effective.

In Sperling's experiment selection of the stimuli for report was successfully achieved if their spatial location was indicated by the cue. The assumption may be made that this represents successful transfer to the short-term store prior to being output as responses. Selection for transfer has also been shown to be possible if the items are specified by their colour, shape or size, but not by category (e.g. letters or digits). This implies that the contents of VIS have not been coded to any significant extent, certainly not to the level of categorization. Coltheart (1972) considered that VIS contains an accurate rendering of the physical properties of the display. Moreover, in so far as the question is given any attention it seems to be assumed that the contents of VIS are formed more or less instantaneously at display onset.

There is less agreement about the nature of the transfer from VIS to subsequent components. Some relevant evidence was obtained by Sperling (1963) with a *backward masking* experiment. This is a procedure in which one stimulus is quickly followed by another at the same location; the perception of the first may be affected if the interval between the onsets of the two stimuli is brief (Kahneman in 1968 provided an explanation of the terminology of masking and a comprehensive review of the evidence and theories).

In this experiment Sperling presented a display of up to six letters (for total report) with a checkerboard pattern to act as the masking stimulus. This was found to be effective in curtailing the life of VIS since at very short delays virtually nothing was reported. But performance increased as the delay increased in such a way that for every 10 ms the mask was delayed, an additional letter was reported, up to a limit of about three to four letters. Sperling therefore concluded that at least the first few items in the display were transferred into a more durable store, possibly coded by this time into an auditory form. This transfer was assumed to be achieved one item at a time. Recall of the items in the display is from this later auditory store, its contents maintained by a process of 'rehearsal'. Some of the evidence for this was that auditory confusions are made in this kind of task (like reporting D instead of T), and subjects declare that they repeat the letters to themselves before reporting. This leads to the chief difficulty with this explanation: the estimated rate of transfer, 100 letters per second, far exceeds the best rate of 6 letters per second which can be reached by subjects rehearsing subvocally (i.e. saying letters to themselves).

A further theoretical development came in 1967 when Sperling proposed that more than one item at a time could be transferred to the auditory store. This was based on the finding that, when the results from the backward masking experiment were looked at more closely, certain effects involving the location of the items in the display began to emerge. It appeared that subjects were quite systematic in reporting the items in an order that corresponded to their position in the display, for example, from left to right, and this showed up in the accuracy with which the items were reported. While this seems like a good case for item-by-item transfer, what was not to be expected was that performance at all positions together improved when the delay of the mask increased. If transfer was strictly one at a time then delaying the mask ought to improve performance on only one item at a time.

As an alternative explanation, Coltheart (1972) suggested that two different kinds of information extraction or encoding operations go on simultaneously as soon as the display is presented. Visual codes of items in the display are formed alongside but independently of a set of name codes. Coltheart assumed that visual coding is rapid but the visual store can only hold a few items, while the naming of the items produces the name codes much more slowly. This enabled him to predict the tendency for performance in the masking experiment to rise rapidly at short delays, but to go on gently rising at longer delays. The current status of theories of VIS is discussed again in the next section.

Masking experiments have also supplied the strongest signs that VIS is at least partly central in origin. It has been shown that the effective duration of VIS can be abbreviated by presenting the display to one eye and the mask to the other. This 'dichoptic' presentation ensures that the action of the mask is post-retinal. However, since dichoptic masking is less severe than the masking produced when mask and display are presented to one (or both) eyes, it seems that there is some retinal contribution to VIS. Whether a functional difference can be identified that corresponds to this apparently dual locus of VIS is not known.

Icons and iconoclasts

It has not been wholly plain sailing for the icon or VIS hypothesis, and a much less sanguine view of the evidence is held by some investigators. Not only are the details of the concept of sensory storage controversial but also the very concept of VIS.

The present situation is crystallized in a series of recent articles which have reviewed the masses of experiments done on the problem in the past fifteen years. Holding (1975a) observed that to a large extent the hypothesis of visual storage and its properties have been accepted 'as a foregone conclusion'. He makes a useful clarification by identifying three aspects of the general VIS hypothesis: that it holds more information than short-term memory, that the availability of information from VIS decreases with time, and that the information held in VIS is uncoded. In the light of the evidence, the only component of this hypothesis that he considers has any merit is that there is a very brief form of visual persistence, and he outlines an alternative explanation for evidence that is generally interpreted in favour of the VIS hypothesis. Coltheart (1975) by way of reply defends 'the conventional popular view of iconic memory', pointing to certain crucial findings that he considers withstand Holding's critique, as well as inadequacies in Holding's alternative explanation. The last word is, at this stage, with Holding's (1975b) brief rejoinder in which he considers the force of Coltheart's proposal of a crucial experiment. It would be impossible for the debate to be summarized in the space available although one or two points will be considered.

In Holding's view the difference in report accuracy under the partial and whole report methods does not have to be interpreted in terms of sensory storage. He claims that the partial report method would be at an advantage if the subject could guess which cue was going to be used on a given trial, since he could then aim his fixation at the position where the cued row would soon appear. It is true that experimenters tend to use 'constrained random orders' for deciding which cue to present when. This usually means that each cue will be given an equal number of times in a given series of trials, so that the assiduous subject could in principle work out which cue would occur on some trials (the 'working out' could be done unconsciously). Holding asked his subjects to guess where the cue was going to come on each trial, and consistent with his argument he found that performance was directly related to the accuracy of anticipating the cue.

There is nevertheless a small residual advantage to the partial report method but Holding interprets this in terms of 'output interference', i.e. the act of producing the responses interferes with the recall of the other items. If only three items have to be produced (under partial report instructions) then they will on average receive less interference than the four or five produced in the whole report condition. And the evidence here too is favourable in the sense that later reported items are indeed less accurate than early ones.

One of the points made by Coltheart in reply is that some crucial experiments remain which seem to resist the cue anticipation and output interference explanations. First, in one of Sperling's experiments the precaution was taken of only balancing the number of trials in the long term (i.e. over two experimental sessions). And the possibility of output interference was ruled out by an experiment by Averbach and Coriell (1961) in which the usual delay effect was found even when only a single cued item had to be reported.

By way of concluding, Coltheart offers a crucial experiment:

> A three by three matrix of letters is presented on each trial for 50 ms and is immediately followed by a visual-noise mask. At display offset a tone is sounded, requesting report of one of the three rows. This partial report condition is compared with a full report condition. Will there be a partial report superiority? (1975, p. 48)

The experiment has yet to be done, but Coltheart suggests the predictions from the two sides are clear, and different. According to the VIS hypothesis, masking will destroy the information in VIS and there will be no partial report advantage. On the other hand, Coltheart argues, masking should have no effect on cue anticipation or output interference, and accordingly there should be the usual advantage to partial report.

But Holding considers the experiment would be unsatisfactory because the mask would reduce performance to a level where differences between the two report methods would be impossibly difficult to detect. So the argument stands and it can perhaps be appreciated why perception researchers don't always sleep easily when two theorists, with closely marshalled facts and arguments, can come up with almost diametrically opposed conclusions about a particular problem. The two positions seem again to show the difficulty of distinguishing between perceptual and response processes.

The icon: a window on the world?

One of the points of using tachistoscopic methods is to rule out eye movements. Of course, the performance of the perceptual system at its limits is itself of interest, and limiting circumstances also allow for differences in performance to show up when they might be concealed under normal viewing conditions. As we have seen, VIS was 'discovered' by this kind of procedure.

Current theories assume that visual stimuli enter the perceptual system via VIS, and Coltheart (1972) has emphasized the relation of visual storage to fixation in reading. The estimated life of VIS does compare quite closely to the duration of a fixation. There has otherwise been little discussion of the generality of tachistoscopic research, or indeed what might be called its ecological validity. It seems to be implicitly assumed that tachistoscopic perception is somehow representative of 'normal perception'. But it is a little odd for the most widely used investigative procedure in visual perception to be one which deprives a man of eye movements, possibly the most basic tools of his visual system. In any event the tachistoscopic task seems to make life unnaturally difficult for the observer, given that his visual world is rarely impaired in this way.

An argument could therefore be made that VIS as demonstrated experimentally is not used in normal perceptual circumstances. There is no direct evidence about this point, although there are findings that suggest that subjects cannot or prefer not to rely on an iconic residue (Barber and Folkard, 1972). Indeed one function of eye movements may be that they serve to cancel the leftovers of VIS; Howarth and Bloomfield (1971) similarly concluded that there may be a clearing mechanism to eliminate interactions between fixations. The disarming possibility presents itself that visual persistence is the result of a 'design defect' in the neural architecture that only shows up under unrepresentative viewing conditions.

Summary

In the course of Chapters 1 to 4 a theoretical approach has been emerging which has been firmly established in the present chapter. Consider the kind of concepts that are used in the following summary statement:

A visual stimulus is represented initially in a short-lived visual information store, whence it is lost unless information is transferred to a later, less ephemeral store where it may be preserved by a process of rehearsal, one possibility being that it is then represented as an auditory code.

The importance of this statement lies not so much in whether it is correct but in the kind of assumptions about perception that it entails and its general conceptual atmosphere. It commits us to the idea that 'information' is being 'processed', it implies that perception consists of a series of 'processes' or 'stages', and it makes use of concepts like 'store' and 'code'. This provides the main conceptual orientation of the rest of the book.

A number of specific issues have been identified which are discussed at length in the next four chapters. There is the question of the usefulness of a multi-stage model of the perceptual system, about which we shall make no conclusive noises but which we offer as a background issue for discussion purposes. More specifically there is the problem of isolating and identifying processes like VIS, and the short-term store. And there is the related issue of the mode of operation of these processes: whether they operate on stimuli one or more at a time, and whether they as processes operate together, in a sequence or in a hierarchy. These questions are taken up directly in Chapter 6 with the problem of information selection.

6
Information selection

An organism is continuously assailed by information. The external bombardment of the senses is only a part of the total set of messages reaching the central nervous system, since to it are added still more signals originating within the body and carrying information about its function. The result could understandably be likened to a cacophony, an incoherent, scrambled mass unlikely to provide a solid base from which to determine interactions with the environment. Though he was making a different point at the time, James' (1890) description of the perceptual world of a baby as a 'booming, buzzing confusion' epitomizes this possible state of affairs.

However, we are seldom led to view our experience of the world in such chaotic terms. Only in some abnormal conditions, including those induced by some drugs like alcohol, does the orderliness of the world inside and out tend to dissolve and leave us in danger of drowning in a disorganized welter of unstructured information. Subjectively, our thoughts may wander from one topic to another, sometimes so fast that vast stretches of remembered time seem to flit past some window of consciousness, but at each instant only one scene is discerned. Even the same object may not be seen in two ways at once. An intricately carved jade chess set could be used to play chess with, and yet appreciation of the carving of the queen and of the pattern of the attack in which she is taking part seem to be incompatible. In this sense the mind appears to favour doing but one thing at a time. Indeed, it may be that this is one of its fundamental limitations (see A5).

This chapter is concerned with differences between the chaos that might be predicted and the reality of experience. It is about the attentional processes which serve to produce this focusing upon selected aspects of the pool of information available to us.

The concept of attention

Like so many words that psychologists have chosen to use in a technical sense, 'attention' is a word with a wide lay currency. Its everyday implications may be indicated by a consideration of the contexts in which it is used. 'Pay attention now', 'Give me your attention', 'Your attention is wandering', 'Attend to your work' – all of these usages suggest an essential element of mental direction and this is, indeed, one of the most important aspects which psychologists have studied. However there are also other aspects of behaviour to which the term has been attached and which can be conceptually distinguished. Moray (1969) considers there to be at least seven distinguishable concepts of attention. These include mental concentration, vigilance, selective attention, selective search, level of arousal or activation, set or preparedness, and analysis-by-synthesis, a process hypothesized by Neisser (1967) to be a fundamental aspect of all perception (Ch. 9).

Selective attention: listening to two messages

It is a peculiarity of the area of enquiry that most research has been done on listening rather than looking. There is no intrinsic reason why audition should be preferred and it seems that the same essential problems of choosing what aspect of the sensory environment to attend to must also apply in vision. Perhaps the crucial thing is that the problem of selecting one auditory message as opposed to another is a more urgent and obvious feature of everyday life. As we saw in Chapter 4, research on looking has concentrated on how information is acquired from a single source, and the competition between alternative sources is a more subtle aspect of the situation.

The ball was set rolling by Cherry in 1953 with an analysis of the so-called 'cocktail party problem'. This is concerned with the problem of maintaining a conversation in a situation where several conversations are taking place. In fact, this can usually be achieved with relatively little difficulty. However, a simple monophonic (as opposed to stereophonic) recording of the same social scene poses enormous problems. What were meaningful, coherent utterances 'in the flesh' are reduced to near gibberish on the recording. There are, of course, several differences between a static microphone and a human listener.

The listener when participating in the party can perhaps orient himself deliberately towards a particular speaker, and even though he lacks a horse's ability to use the pinnae of his ears like an ear trumpet he may be able to maximize the volume he receives from that particular speaker. The microphone lacks such directional sensitivity and instead tends to respond to sound waves reaching it from all directions as a simple function of their intensity. However, more than this is necessary to unravel the complex interrelated sound patterns to produce coherent speech. Analysis shows that there seem to be a number of additional pieces of information which go to make comprehension possible. For example, it helps to know who is speaking, that is, where they are and something about the general properties of their voice. It is also useful to know what they are talking about. This suggests that had the sound recording been in stereo the difficulties would be reduced – and, indeed, this is the case. An analogous visual situation is watching the conjurer despite the fascination of the conjurer's assistant's legs, although this has yet to be dignified as a research project.

The 'cocktail party' issue was one, but only one, of the primary stimuli to research on attention. There are other, non-social, situations in which one message has to be distinguished from others (for example, the task of an air-traffic controller monitoring one among several radio messages). The Applied Psychology Unit at Cambridge conducted a number of studies on this question during the early 1950s using a more deliberately controlled situation than a cocktail party. These experiments mostly involved presenting to a subject two short messages, each often consisting of only three digits (or similar items). These items were presented rapidly in pairs so that all six were presented in a matter of three to five seconds. The members of each pair were presented simultaneously. The subjects either had to repeat back all the digits presented or just those comprising one message. In the latter case each message was preceded by an identifying 'call-sign' and only after the messages were presented were the subjects given the call-sign of the message to be reported. Many of these experiments were summarized by Broadbent (1958).

One of the main questions concerned the effect of mode of presentation. Sometimes subjects wore headphones and received both messages through both ears (monaural presentation), and sometimes each ear received a different message (dichotic presentation). When these kinds of presentation were compared, it was found that dichotic stimulation led to vastly superior performance in separating the messages for selective report, or in total recall if that was required.

Broadbent and his colleagues conducted a large series of experiments of this kind, varying the source of messages, their speed of presentation, the voices speaking them and their structure. A number of basic regularities were observed. Striking effects on performance were achieved by effecting some kind of physical distinction between the simultaneously presented messages. This could be done by varying the auditory location of the messages by dichotic presentation or separated loudspeakers. Functional separation of messages could also be effected by manipulating the general frequency of the voices. For example, a male and a female voice made two messages separable as did the selective filtering out of treble frequencies from one message and bass frequencies from the other. Somewhat less dramatic, but still of considerable effect, was the category of items constituting the message. For example, if one message were ABC and another 123, separation was readily achieved. In fact if there was a category relation between items in different messages in a dichotic task, this often overrode their physical relatedness. Thus there was a very real risk of 'cross-talk' if message 1B3 was presented to one ear and A2C to the other. The subject generally reported categorically homogeneous strings, 123 and ABC.

One significant feature of the results is that when both messages had to be recalled, the first to be reported was the more accurate. Since the items of the messages arrive together and can only be spoken one after the other, some work is necessary in scheduling the order in which they are to be output. It follows therefore that some system must intervene in addition to an information selection system. So these investigations were bound to run into the now familiar snag of distinguishing between perception and memory effects.

Switching theory

The Cambridge experiments led Broadbent to develop a model which sought to accommodate the general findings concerning performance with simultaneously presented messages. Its essential features are shown in Figure 6.1.

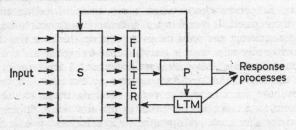

Fig. 6.1 *Broadbent's model of information processing of parallel inputs (after Broadbent, 1958)*

The model comprises two essential systems connected by a *filter* device which controls the flow of information between them. Input information flows into the S-system from the sensory processes. This system was conceived of as a *sensory store*, essentially *pre-categorical* in nature. That is, its contents are not subjected to any complex coding or categorization but rather remain in a raw sensory state: there is an obvious similarity with the VIS of Chapter 5. The system capable of carrying out complex coding, categorization and translation is the P-system. While it is not a requirement of the model that any aspect of its operation be open to introspective scrutiny, it is implicit that no part of the model *prior* to the P-system could give rise to conscious data. The literal labels of the boxes probably derive from their notional functions: S stands for sensory storage, P for perception.

Items of information entering the P-system either exit via the selective filter, or 'decay' and eventually cease to exist. It is as if the S-system were an acid bath which destroys its contents unless they are rescued fairly quickly. The selective filter is the rescue route and any items it selects pass directly to the P-system for analysis and disposal. Three different routes lead out from the P-system but they are not strictly alternatives. Items may be recirculated to the S-system, or placed into long-term store (see A6), or lead to some sort of response. Any one or more of these could happen. It may be noted that the recirculation of items through the S- and P-systems offers a representation of what can be thought of as *rehearsal*. The role of rehearsal here is to offset the 'decay' that would otherwise be suffered by items held in the S-system.

For the present the critical component of this model is the filter. Broadbent conceived of it as a switch selecting items by their 'channel' membership. *Channel* has proved to be an elusive concept and must be given some explanation. We shall provisionally take it in a general sense to signify something like an attribute shared by a set of items that can be selected by the filter. Such items are selected by the filter – because they have this common property – and then pass to the P-system. Since the filter represents the selectional system in attention, its mode of operation is crucial, and this is discussed a little later. It will transpire that not all selectable attributes can sensibly be identified with channels. We shall nevertheless assume for the present that the two ideas are equivalent. What attributes, then, are in fact selectable?

The evidence discussed above suggests that the relevant features for selection include the anatomical site of arrival of the input ('left ear versus right ear' is the one studied, but 'eye versus ear' is an obvious candidate also). The concept of channel originally seems to have been adopted when the principal distinction was in terms of the different anatomical routes provided by the two ears. Subsequently the defining features of a channel have been broadened until the anatomical component plays a very minor role.

One very dramatic demonstration of the subtlety of the channel concept is provided by the demonstration of the three-eared man. A little background may be helpful in understanding it. If a pure tone is presented to *both* ears, it is not heard as a pair of tones one at each ear but as a single tone with a particular location in space. Its apparent location is determined in part by the relative intensity of sound at the two ears. If the left ear is louder it will be located in the left ear, if the right ear is louder, then in the right. If equal intensities are presented to the two ears the sound is 'heard' to emanate from some point in the middle of the head.

Treisman (1964a) made use of the phenomenon in an experiment in which she played one message to the left ear, a different message to the right and a third equally to both ears. Subjects could selectively listen to any one of the three messages. Clearly this would not be possible if the basis for their selection was to 'listen' to one ear rather than the other. The selective mechanism must instead be operating with a more sophisticated code than anatomical site. This suggests that the apparent location of the message is more crucial than its anatomical locus. The evidence also showed that physical characteristics of the message, such as its typical sound frequency, enable the message to be selected.

But selection can also be achieved through the semantic attributes of the message and this is really where the trouble starts. The problem arises because if the S-system is conceived of as a pre-processing store it is implausible to assert that selection of information from that store is on the basis of a distinction that could only be arrived at after a considerable degree of processing. The anatomical specification of channel poses relatively few problems of this kind. It would be straightforward to conceive of the input to one ear being stored in the S-system in a way which simply reflected ear of arrival. General features of the message such as its dominant sound frequencies or location might also be stored in a relatively simple way. But the *semantic* definition of a channel raises problems of a different order. It is hard to envisage a system that could establish the theme of a message without analysing it. It would seem that the Broadbent conceptualization of the S-system and its associated filter needs some reconsideration if 'semantic' channels are to be plausibly incorporated within it.

The second basic question concerns the *manner* in which the selective filter operates. Its function is described as similar to a rotary switch which is successively connected to different channels. Only one channel is connected at a particular instant and only a connected channel can feed information through to the P-system. Clearly, one important question concerns the factors which determine which channel is connected. An unacceptable solution would be any one that somehow demanded a superordinate system or agent to turn the switch to the desired channel, since it would then be necessary to describe the mode of operation of the decision taken in the superordinate system. This kind of homunculus (or 'little man in the head') approach is dangerous since in no time at all one is on the endless road of an infinite regress (little men operating on other little men ...). Clearly, what is required is a system which does not necessitate the intervention of an external decision-maker. There are a number of possible solutions.

The simplest scheme would be for the filter to switch regularly to each channel in a cyclic order. The selective aspect of attention could be achieved by arranging for connections to some channels to be maintained *for disproportionate lengths of time*. With this scheme it is necessary to specify the factors which determine why some channels are preferentially sampled for longer time intervals. However, even with this scheme it is still axiomatic that all channels are sampled periodically. This is necessary to provide an opportunity for attention to be redirected in favour of some new informational source.

Broadbent has listed the characteristics of channels which are supposed to lead to their preferential selection. These include physical intensity, novelty, and time since channel last sampled, high frequency sounds rather than low, sound rather than visual stimuli. In addition channels take priority if they convey information which is particularly important to the organism. Importance in this case is defined by the motivational need state of the organism.

This conception of a selective filter switch appears to offer an explanation of the principal phenomena derived from the early dichotic listening experiments. One issue that arises is that of *the time it takes to switch from one channel to another*. This problem seems to be a difficult one to solve. However, if the model is to have credibility it would seem necessary to put some limits on its value. Experiments in which a speech message was switched from ear to ear showed there was a loss of intelligibility when the switching rate was about three times per second, and this was the value Broadbent originally settled on. But there is also evidence that certain components of the speech signal are distorted in the process, so that it may not be a simple matter of the switching rate being critical *per se*. There are also so many different estimates of switching rates that it seems unlikely that a single value could be agreed upon.

Attenuator theory

In a series of papers since 1960 an attempt has been made by Treisman to reconcile the switching filter model with some awkward findings about the amount of information subjects manage to derive from a non-attended channel.

She has adopted the '*shadowing*' technique described by Cherry (1953) as her principal methodology. In this paradigm subjects are played a tape-recording of (usually) a prose passage and required to repeat it orally. That is, they simply have to say what they hear. Simultaneously, other information may be presented. If dichotic presentation is used, as it often is, the message to be shadowed is presented to one ear while the ancillary or secondary message is presented to the other. Interest centres around the influence on performance of the content of the secondary message, and the extent to which subjects notice and subsequently report its character.

In his original report Cherry (1953) reported that his subjects were afterwards able to say surprisingly little about the secondary message. They knew the sex of the speaker, and whether the message consisted of words rather than non-speech sounds, but apparently they were unable to report anything of its semantic content or even the language in which it was spoken. However, Cherry also reported that if the two messages were identical but staggered in time the subjects realized this. Treisman's subjects also became aware of this identity of meaning if one message was a translation of the other.

A particularly dramatic effect reported by Moray (1959) is that subjects sometimes respond to the occurrence of their own name in the secondary message. In addition, Treisman discovered that on some occasions subjects, while shadowing a piece of prose, would introduce words from the secondary message when they fitted into the sense and syntax of the primary message.

Treisman (1964b) concluded that the concept of an all-or-none switch of the kind postulated by Broadbent was unduly stretched by these findings. She proposed instead that the selective mechanism acted by a process of *attenuation*. This attenuation consists of a hierarchy of analysing mechanisms tuned to progressively more complex aspects of the signal. Preliminary analyses would establish the physical characteristics of the items and later ones would eventually determine their full meaning. At an intermediate stage items would be evaluated for their importance even before their full meaning had been determined. At each stage of this hierarchy an effective decision could be taken whether or not to proceed further with the analysis of that item.

This new conceptualization avoids some of the rather knotty problems of the Broadbent model. There is no filter to be switched between channels so the specification of switching time is not an issue. Treisman's model also gets over the problem of how to specify a channel. This is avoided by considering a hierarchy of analytical processes rather than a single analysis which in Broadbent's scheme is the responsibility of the P-system. Whereas the switch selected one channel at a time, the attenuator gives a graduated response in relation to all attributes.

Response selection theory
In 1963 Deutsch and Deutsch, having regard to the same evidence that led Treisman to formulate her model, produced one of their own. In essence they argue that reports that subjects can perceive the verbal content of rejected messages imply that the selection must occur *after* rather than before a full analysis of inputs. In other words, all input signals are fully analysed. The function of the selective filter is to determine which of these fully analysed signals should lead to a response, and that decision is supposed to be determined by the momentary relative importance of the responses. At first sight this seems to be easy to distinguish from Treisman's model and there is some research that set out to do this.

Perception versus response
Treisman and Geffen (1967) reported an experiment which was designed as a critical test between Treisman's theory and that of the Deutschs. In essence Treisman conceives of the system as consisting of two major processing systems, one which analyses as far as the verbal characteristics of sensory input and a later system which defines responses. The two theories are distinguished by the location of the selective mechanism. In Treisman's model the attenuator is placed before the verbal analysis system. In the Deutschs' model it

appears between the verbal analysis processor and that which defines responses. This contrast is depicted in Figure 6.2.

The diagram seems to indicate that a simple distinction is implied by the two models and, therefore, that a clear choice could be made on the basis of experimental evidence. This is what Treisman and Geffen sought to do. The primary task (on channel 1) was to shadow a passage from Conrad's novel *Lord Jim*. This was presented to one ear while another

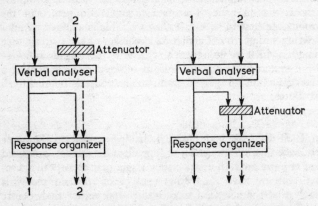

Fig. 6.2 *Representations of Treisman's model (on the left) and Deutsch and Deutsch's model (on the right) of selective attention (after Treisman and Geffen, 1967)*

Treisman's model shows that the power of response 2 depends upon the input route which leads to it. The Deutschs' model, however, predicts that the input route will not affect the power of the response.

passage from the same text was presented to the other ear. Both were doctored slightly by the insertion of a number of target words. These were words defined to the subject in advance, and he was instructed to tap the table in front of him if he heard them.

The results showed quite clearly that when the target word was presented in the primary message it was much more likely to be followed by the tapping response than when it was presented in the secondary message. The percentages of correct detections were dramatically different. Target words in the primary channel were detected about 86 per cent of the time whereas target words on the secondary (unshadowed) channel were detected only 8 per cent of the time. Such a difference when compared with the expectation shown in Figure 6.2 clearly seems to support the Treisman model rather than that of the Deutschs.

Furthermore, expressing their results in terms of the parameters of signal detection theory (Ch. 3), Treisman and Geffen found that the poorer detection rate for the tapping stimulus was wholly attributable to a reduction in d' (sensitivity), there being no change in β (criterion). The reported values for d' for stimuli on the unshadowed channel were about half those for the shadowed ear. This suggests that something intervened between stimulus reception and decision that reduced the strength of the evidence provided by the stimulus. This appears to be an instance of the operation of differential attenuation as postulated in the Treisman model.

Treisman and Riley (1969) conducted a further experiment in which the subject stopped shadowing whenever the secondary task called for a response. An important methodological innovation was the use of a computer to ensure that the onsets and offsets of the stimuli to one ear were synchronized with those to the other. The subject was presented dichotically with two strings of digits intermingled with occasional letters. His instructions were to shadow the digits to one (the attended) ear, and at the same time to report when a letter occurred in either ear.

There was virtually perfect performance at detecting the letters (99 per cent detection) when the letters and digits were spoken in different voices. This high detection rate was achieved regardless of whether the target letter was spoken on the shadowed or unshadowed channel. It suggests that general sound frequency of the voice is detected by means of a superficial analysis completed very early in the processing sequence and prior to any noticeable degree of attenuation.

Performance was considerably poorer when the same voice spoke both the letters and digits. In this case, letters were detected rather more than twice as often on the shadowed channel (76 per cent of the time) compared with the unshadowed channel (33 per cent of the time). The separation of the two channels seems to have been less clear-cut in this experiment. This is supported by the far from perfect shadowing performance (70 per cent).

Perhaps channel identification is easier if there are relatively frequent occasions when only one channel is active. The careful synchronization of the stimuli in this experiment would eliminate such occurrences. One possibility is that there was no way for the subjects to discriminate between the apparent locations of the two messages.

Capacity sharing

It was suggested by Taylor, Lindsay and Forbes (1967) that an information processing system of fixed capacity would share out this capacity when dealing with several sources. Using an index of total capacity based on the d' measure, they found that in practice there was a capacity loss of 15 per cent in a sharing task as compared to the summed capacities obtained in concentrated conditions. A second interesting result was that the capacity needs of sharing between channels *within* a modality are no different from sharing *between* modalities.

These findings are consistent with Moray's (1967) suggestion that the information processor can elect to work in several ways, but that some work-schemes imply an organizational load reducing the capacity available for actually processing incoming information. It is rather as if some capacity is busy directing information traffic rather than getting on with the substantive job of processing it. One of the essential problems in the area is to give a detailed account of how the organizational capacity is spent. So far research has provided relatively little information about how the total system alters its characteristic mode of working.

Further developments

A number of recent developments attribute to the memory process a major role in the matter of selection. Working along the lines of the Deutschs' model, Shiffrin and his colleagues assert that subjects are quite incapable of directing attention to input channels until these channels have been identified by the nature of the information they carry. This view, which pushes the locus of the mechanism of selection deeper into the information processing system, is elaborated by Shiffrin and Grantham (1974).

Other research has concentrated on the fate of unattended material in terms of its availability for subsequent recall. In the early studies using shadowing, subjects were typically unable to report very much about the secondary message. Later experiments in examining recall have naturally emphasized the role of memory and the nature of the storage medium (Bryden, 1971).

Though this would seem to be the moment for a conclusion, one is not possible. Many of the experimental procedures that have been employed in studying this problem are imperfect. It is especially difficult to overcome the problem that in a dichotic listening experiment subjects may not follow the instructions to listen to one source only. Even when computer-aided synchronization has been used it is often feared that subjects may 'switch' between sources. These problems are particularly severe when verbal stimuli are used instead of very brief pure tones, and this makes the evidence for semantic analysis of unattended items even more precarious. Perhaps it makes the problem more complex rather than simpler, but the main positive indications that seem inescapable are that selective attention is not simply a perceptual phenomenon.

A kind of progressive selection imposed on input information similar to Treisman's progressive attenuation process seems to be the best bet. A conceptualization of perceptual and memory processes as continuous with one another, with attention as an elastic band which may be wrapped around them at any point, may be more profitable than one in which perception and memory are distinct and have distinctive properties.

7
Pattern recognition

Intriguing as they are, the problems of search, selection and acquisition are not the end of our line of enquiry. So far the perceptual system has only been persuaded to find its source of information: it remains for it to do something with it. Its captive data have to be submitted to further processing.

Having located a visual object, the next task is to identify it – this is more generally referred to as the problem of pattern recognition. This is not to say that it is easy, or ultimately sensible, to make a distinction between the operations of selection and recognition. The guidance of the selectional apparatus has to be explained and this seems likely to involve the action and interaction of mechanisms at different levels in the nervous system. A complete model may have to treat these nominally separate components as a unity. So the business of this chapter is with pattern recognition. We begin with a favourite problem of the pattern recognition theorist.

In Figure 7.1 we have collected together some examples of how black print can be deposited on a two-dimensional surface (this sheet of paper) to give visual patterns that have the letter name A. Taking any pair it is easy enough to spot differences between them, and yet all the letters are somehow treated as belonging to the same class. How do we recognize them all as As? We shall look at two alternatives to begin with as a kind of feasibility study. This will also give us an opportunity to discover more about pattern recognition.

Perhaps we refer them all to a 'standard' A. Suppose, for

example, we take the circled letter A in the top right-hand corner of Figure 7.1 as our standard. One approach would be to use the standard as a *template* to be placed on top of any 'input' character. The input is 'recognized' (i.e. given the same name) as the template if they can be brought into exact register with one another. It must be possible for the template to be used all over the page (insensitivity to position). And

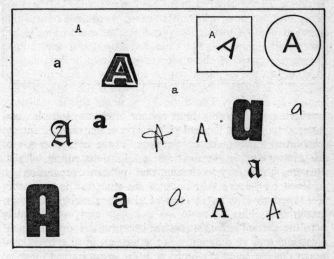

Fig. 7.1 *The letter 'A' and some of its variations*

to 'recognize' its tilted near-neighbour in the square the template (or the input) must be able to rotate about an axis (insensitivity to orientation). To deal with the smaller A in the square the template must be able to shrink (insensitivity to size). Insensitivity to position, size and orientation changes could conceivably be achieved by some kind of preprocessing operation, designed to regularize the input relative to the template. In the case of orientation the 'top' and 'bottom' of each pattern would have to be 'known' to the preprocessor for this to work. (It is understandably hard to appreciate that all this presents a problem until it is realized that one 'knows' about this by courtesy of one's perceptual system.)

But this can only be part of the story: to recognize the

other characters in Figure 7.1 we shall need additional standards because the one we have chosen will not match many of them even if we allow for all manner of geometrical distortions. Certainly a lower case 'a' and the variety of hand-written 'a's will necessitate additional templates. It is partly because of the storage demands required by a template-matching system that it has not had popular support; there would simply have to be too many templates for each letter (let alone all the other patterns we can recognize). It is also difficult to see how novel instances of A could be correctly classified without instruction – and yet there are likely to be patterns in Figure 7.1 that have never been met before and yet are recognized by the reader as As without hesitation.

A clue to the problem can be found by considering how difficult it is to describe the ways in which the characters in Figure 7.1 do vary. The difficulty of doing this in ordinary language may impose a limit on our attempts at explaining pattern recognition. One solution is to consider the elementary components that make up patterns. These components are also known as *features* and some of the most successful approaches to date hypothesize that pattern recognition is achieved by *feature analysis*. Feature analysis theories have been used to give an account of character recognition and speech recognition.

In the written language one 'natural' unit in terms of which a message can be segmented is the letter. But in spoken language the segmentation problem is far greater since there is no obvious 'natural' unit. Examination of the physical wave-forms that speech signals consist of indicates that there are no gaps between letters (or even words) to serve as analogues of the spaces between letters. Therefore, it is easier to appreciate the necessity of specifying functional units for the purpose of understanding speech recognition. This should warn us at the same time that the functional unit in word recognition and reading may not be the naturally obvious candidate (letter or word). Recognition of individual characters poses a similar problem.

We might begin with the *phoneme* as the basic unit in speech recognition. This is the smallest speech sound which by itself can change the meaning of a word, e.g. the *ee* sound in 'seat' and the *i* sound in 'sit' are phonemes. Two phonemes which are represented identically in written English are the

92

two different initial phonemes in *th*en and *th*is; similarly, the central phonemes in t*o*y and t*o*p are both represented in the written language by the letter *o*. But although phonemes are convenient functional units, it has proved difficult to specify them physically and this has cautioned some theorists against treating them as the building-block of speech recognition.

Jakobson, Fant and Halle (1951) suggested that the phonemes themselves could be represented in terms of *distinctive features*: these were a range of dimensions like nasal–oral, continuous–interrupted, voice–unvoiced and so on. These dimensions are based on considerations to do with the vocal mechanics involved in producing the sounds. The *ss* sound in 'loss' is unvoiced because the vocal chords are not operated while making the sound; the *n* in 'song' is nasal while the *s* in the same word is oral for fairly obvious reasons. The air-flow is interrupted in sounding the *ch* in 'choice', it is sounded orally, and it is unvoiced. In contrast, the *sh* in 'shop' involves no interruption in the air-flow, although it too is sounded orally and unvoiced. In this scheme a unique description of each of the English phonemes can be given. It should be noted that it is inevitably difficult to specify these speech units physically since they are sub-units of the phoneme. Nevertheless, feature analysis theory has received a good deal of attention.

Recognition of a phoneme is achieved by noting the presence or absence of each particular distinctive feature in the input signal and hence arriving at a description of the signal, perhaps in the form of a *list* of feature values (present/absent). In conjunction with a set of standard feature-lists the label of the phoneme can be retrieved. Each distinctive feature enables a subset of the alternative phonemes to be eliminated.

Gibson (1969) described an analogous attempt to develop a specification of capital letters in terms of distinctive features. Several classes of features were used including straight lines (horizontal, vertical, left-sloping, right-sloping), curved lines (open, closed), intersection, symmetry and discontinuity (horizontal or vertical). The eventual list of features enables each capital letter to be uniquely specified. Each distinctive feature again enables a subset of the letter alternatives to be ruled out. Thus for the feature 'horizontal straight line' the letters B C D I J K M N O P Q R S U V W X Y are eliminated in its absence. Of the remaining alternatives A E

F G H L T Z only G is eliminated if the next test is for 'curvedness'. The specifications arrived at are unique for these fairly simple characters, but they are not if more elaborate typefaces are allowed.

To test whether the chosen feature list is used in discriminating between letters, a confusion matrix was obtained. The number of occasions a given letter was mistaken for any other was recorded; this was done by presenting each letter as the standard in a multiple-choice task with the other letters serving as the 'distractors'. For each letter the correlation was found between the number of features it had in common with every other letter and the number of occasions it was mistaken for them. The prediction was that, for example, since E and F share several features while E and V have none in common the former pair are more likely to be confused than the latter. This was borne out but the evidence was not strong. Of course, in a fairly general sense the contours of E and F overlap more than E and V, and a template-matching system could be expected, if it tolerated some discrepancies, to confuse F for E more often than V for E. It is of interest, therefore, that a measure of contour overlap on balance correlated with confusion errors less strongly than the number of shared features.

The disappointing performance of the distinctive features scheme for classifying letters could be interpreted against the feature analysis theory of human pattern recognition, but in practice other conclusions are preferred. What could be in error is the detail of the classification scheme or the assumed features. In fact the confusion error data against which the predictions of the feature analysis model were tested could provide ideas about how to revise the scheme. In practice theoretical alternatives to a feature analysis approach are not easy to come by, and psychologists have pressed on with the development and testing of feature analysis theory.

Feature analysis has in principle a number of advantages. In Gibson's scheme as few as ten distinctive features were needed to give a unique specification of a capital letter of a simplified typeface. Furthermore, if the pattern recognizer can make use of probabilities it is not necessary for all the distinctive feature values to be known. It may be possible to eliminate many alternatives on the basis of two or three features; the final choice among the remaining alternatives could be guided by data about their probabilities. This would be most effective if it was in the form of transitional probability information (i.e. probabilities taking the prior context into account). This tends to make the theory more complicated, and the behaviour of the system less error-free. But the first is surely inevitable, and second is only realistic in view of the confusion mistakes that are made in discriminating between letters. If the pattern recognizer can also receive feedback about its performance then it can check the adequacy of a list of feature values for the purpose of identifying a new stimulus category (the symbol θ, say). It can now exhibit *learning*.

The additional complications are not difficult to justify since they implicate mechanisms which are essentially separate from the pattern recognition system. Thus it has to be supplied with a source of probability information (in secondary/long-term memory; see A6) and a decision-making capability. It has not been suggested that it be equipped with the ability to generate new distinctive features. This is something of a drawback unless we assume that the necessary perceptual equipment is entirely 'wired-in' and is brought into play only when ultimately necessary (see Ch. 2).

The search for elementary features

The task of enumerating the elementary features in visual pattern recognition has been tackled on various fronts at the same time. Logical analysis of particular classes of patterns like letters and digits has been used to justify the inclusion of the 'symmetry' feature for character recognition, but this is not the kind of ultimate justification that one looks for and it can hardly count as 'evidence' in favour of such a feature analyser. Neurophysiological observations about the operation of feature analysers in the early stages of processing (Ch. 2) provide a sounder source of evidence. It may have been noticed incidentally that such analysers could be thought of as miniature templates; the difference between template-matching and feature analysis may therefore be a matter of level of conceptual analysis.

The success of neuroanatomists and neurophysiologists in mapping out information routes and processing mechanisms in the preliminary stages of visual analysis is particularly impressive. But the more central stages of the visual process have yet to be penetrated, so there is no immediate prospect that pattern recognition can be explained in physiological terms. This would in any case be premature given that the psychological issues are themselves only now becoming clear.

What are the contents of the perceptual tool-kit that could be useful in pattern recognition? By monitoring the electrical activity in single cells in various layers of the visual cortex of rabbits, cats and monkeys (Barlow and Levick, 1965; Hubel and Wiesel, 1962, 1968) it is known that there are detectors of various physical properties like edges, slits and bars. The responses of these detectors or analysers depend critically on the orientation of the stimulus, and they may also be maximally sensitive to movement in a particular direction. In the outer layers of the visual cortex the detectors (simple cells) seem to be responsible for quite narrowly defined retinal areas. At the next level in the cortex are the complex cells, with essentially the same characteristics as the simple cells but their response is less bound by the position of the stimulus on the retina. Beyond this are the hyper-complex cells which have an additional selectivity of response to line length and edge width. At this level angle detectors have also been observed. So the basic tools seem to vary in their generality and flexibility of response. They are reassuringly consistent with the kinds of feature detectors that one might be persuaded to design into a biological pattern recognition device on the basis of logical analysis.

But we know little about the involvement of these detectors in complex pattern recognition. Size-specific and position-specific responding exist more or less alongside size-independent and position-independent responding. Therefore the potential seems to exist at a primitive level for the visual system to discriminate between stimuli varying in these characteristics and also to treat them as equivalent with very little additional processing. But this is frankly speculative, and while speculation is free it may be misleading.

Psychologists were quick to make capital out of neuro-physiological discoveries about the nature of image coding in the visual system, although some applications were over-enthusiastic (Uttal, 1971). A contemporary view is put by Haber and Hershenson (1973), who present an information-processing model for visual perception. A temptation is to assume that in this model the first of several central representations of the stimulus consists of the 'visual features that are the outputs of the receptive field organization of the cortex'. But Haber and Hershenson resist the temptation, not wishing to consider the search for features closed, nor in view of the continuing evolution of neurophysiological research overly to constrain their own theoretical options. We should also remind ourselves that the relevance of this research for human pattern recognition has yet to be directly established.

Further evidence of feature analysers

Visual after-effects provide one source of evidence relating to feature analysers. An example of these involves the use of black and white patterns of stripes, known as gratings for obvious reasons; see Figure 2.1(b). The concept of a *contrast threshold* must be clarified first: this refers to the luminance difference at a boundary which is necessary for the boundary to be detected. For a grating pattern it is the luminance difference between dark and light bars needed for the grating to be visible (at low contrast levels it is seen as an even grey patch). If a grating of a particular spatial frequency (defined as the number of repetitions of the black-white pattern per visual angle) is inspected for a minute or so then the contrast threshold for gratings of similar frequency is impaired, but there is no effect if the test grating is of a sufficiently different spatial frequency. But in the latter case the *apparent* spatial frequency is affected: a 'broader' pattern (lower spatial frequency) seems even broader, and a narrower (higher spatial frequency) seems even narrower. Moreover these perceptual effects are orientation-specific: adaptation (via prolonged inspection) to a horizontal grating does not affect the contrast threshold of vertical gratings, nor their apparent spatial frequency. This may be significant since the neurophysical evidence on size (and spatial-frequency) detectors shows that they too are orientation-specific. These findings 'suggest that the visual system of man is organized somewhat similarly to that of the cat and monkey' (Blakemore and Nachmias, 1971).

This problem of organizational similarity has also been tackled using the *evoked cortical potential* as a 'linkage technique'. The evoked cortical potential refers to the change in electrical activity of the cortex which is contingent on the presentation of a stimulus. A technical problem of measuring this evoked potential arises because it may be swamped by the ongoing spontaneous electrical activity in the brain. This is overcome by taking the average of a number of cortical responses. The assumption is that a sample of spontaneous activity is not linked to the stimulus presentation, and so by being averaged together with other samples it tends to cancel out, leaving the average effect specifically due to the stimulus. The resulting wave-form is the average evoked cortical potential. Plainly it implicates the activity of a mass of cortical neurons, being measured usually via electrodes placed on the scalp. The issue here is whether it can provide evidence to bridge the gulf between the neurophysiological and psychological levels. Campbell and Maffei (1970) have shown that the amplitude of the evoked potential varies systematically with the contrast of a grating pattern. In addition the amplitude of the evoked potential decreased when an adapting pattern of similar orientation was used, but there was no effect on the amplitude if the orientation was more than 15 degrees different from the evoking pattern. This led Campbell and Maffei to conclude that 'in man there exist neurons highly selective to both orientation and spatial frequency'.

Machines and pattern recognition

Machines have been built that can recognize simple characters like the stylized ones on bank cheques. Thus pattern recognition is also the province of certain engineers and computer scientists. Other tasks that have been tackled include recognition of handwritten characters, speech, connected prose, musical notation, clouds, disease symptoms and visual scenes. The goal of some of this work has been to build a machine to do these tasks. The principles built into such machines may naturally be of interest to psychologists. There is a two-way traffic here since the machine designer may well turn to psychology as a source of ideas.

Other research has been concerned to build a machine (or equivalently to program a computer) to simulate the way a human recognizes a given object or event. The machine or program can be thought of as a model or theory of pattern recognition and this approach is clearly of particular interest to psychologists. Some indeed have been attracted to this kind of research because of the extraordinary rigour that such theories possess: all the theorist's assumptions have to be stated unambiguously for the theory to be implemented in this form. This makes life hard for the theorist but the advantages of being clear and explicit about one's assumptions are not to be gainsaid. The research on machine recognition is discussed by Uhr (1966).

Pandemonium

In Figure 7.2 is a schematic version of a pattern recognition model (Selfridge, 1959) which has had considerable appeal among psychologists. It was successfully implemented for

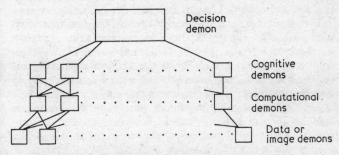

Fig. 7.2 *Pandemonium: a model for pattern recognition*
(after Selfridge, 1959)

machine recognition of morse code and a small set of handwritten characters (Selfridge and Neisser, 1960). For reasons which will become clear Selfridge called it a Pandemonium model. The components of Pandemonium are for metaphorical purposes called 'demons'. The input to Pandemonium is inspected first by a collection of mechanisms responsible for extracting data from the stimulus. These are the data or *image* demons, and they are concerned with primitive feature analysis; the simple stimulus properties they deal with could include hooks, bars, concavity, horizontal lines, vertical lines, oblique lines, closed loops and so on. A given demon has the task of 'shrieking' in proportion to the amount of his assigned stimulus property in the input.

At the next level in this hierarchical system is a set of demons to carry out certain common computational opera-

99

tions on the output from the lower level. There may be *computational* demons with the task of assessing the presence of both bar and closed loop, counting the number of free ends and so on. The results of their calculations pass to the *cognitive* demons in the layer immediately beyond them. They in their turn are specialized; one cognitive demon, for instance, may be responsible for the letter A and will shriek according to how A-like is the input to him. At the top of this diabolical hierarchy is the *decision* demon who listens to the screams of his cognitive demons and chooses the loudest of them as the name of the input character. The weights attached by any demon to his inputs may be modified in the light of experience and this enables Pandemonium to learn. A shortcoming of the model is that it is not equipped to generate new demons at any level.

Pandemonium deals with many alternatives simultaneously. Thus, it checks whether the input signal is A at the same time as checking whether it is B, C, D and so on. This simultaneity of processing activities is the mark of a *parallel processing* system. It may be contrasted with a *serial processing* system in which only one activity is ongoing at a time.

So Pandemonium is a parallel processing system and it operates on the basis of feature analysis. Although feature analysis and parallel processing are combined in this model this is not a logical necessity and other combinations of mechanism and processing mode are possible (e.g. serial template-matching etc.) if not plausible.

Neisser (1967) argued that the early stages of pattern recognition are achieved by a system like Pandemonium. For example, one of his experiments suggested that scanning times in visual search depend on the featural similarity of targets and background. If the target was Q then search was much quicker if the background consisted of angular letters than if they were round letters. For Z as the target, scanning was faster in a context of round letters than in a context of angular letters. This seems to implicate feature analysis because it suggests that more processing is needed when target and background stimuli have common features. But the explanation is not very clear beyond this. The parallel processing assumption is discussed in Chapter 8.

We said that Pandemonium could cope with perceptual learning effects and a neat demonstration of these effects is found in an experiment by Rabbitt (1967). The task was to sort cards bearing a set of letters into piles depending on which target letter was on them. After a number of trials at this task, the cards were changed so that although the target was the same the background items were different. The notion was that the subject would slow down if he had come to rely on particular features of the background items to make the target-background discrimination. This was confirmed and the decrease in performance on the transfer trials tended to increase as the number of training trials increased. A second, more direct, sign of the involvement of feature analysis was that for targets C and O, whereas there was no slowing down when transferring from a context of angular letters (A, E, F, H, I, K, L) to a context of different angular letters (M, N, T, V, W, X, Y), there was a slowing down if the new context was of round letters (B, D, G, J, P, Q, S). This suggests the discrimination of target from non-target was achieved on the basis of information about straight-line features.

The Pandemonium system offers the prospect that a task could be achieved with very little involvement of the higher levels in the processing hierarchy. An item may be classified as a non-target on the basis of minimal feature information. It seems to follow that certain kinds of classification could in principle be achieved without the identification of the item in question. This interesting possibility is supported by the reports of Neisser's subjects that they did not see the non-target items clearly:

> Subjects insist that they do not 'see' individual letters at all, that everything is a blur from which the target 'stands out'. (Neisser, 1967, p. 70)

However, other evidence discussed in Chapter 9, that classification can indeed precede identification, raises problems for feature analytic explanations.

Other theories and other problems

Other theoretical views of pattern recognition are discussed at a more advanced level by Reed (1973). A cogent argument against a simple feature analysis theory, with a good deal of support in this chapter, is that recognition involves more than a mere listing of features, and that relations between them have to be taken into account. This more complete specification is referred to as a 'structural description' by Sutherland (1973). Other theoretical developments, basically guided by the feature analysis approach, are discussed in Chapter 9.

Restricting ourselves to the 'simple' problems of speech and character recognition has perhaps concealed the enormity of the task facing the pattern recognition theorist. We recognize words, people (by their faces, voices, handwriting, gaits and footsteps), melodies, flowers, facial expressions and so on. Some people in addition learn to interpret X-ray photographs, styles of music, aeroplane silhouettes, blips on a radar screen, irregularities in automobile engine sounds etc. Perception psychology has a good deal of business to attend to! It has tended to ignore the larger questions – perhaps on the little-acorns-into-big-oak-trees-grow principle – unless there are pressing practical issues involved.

In this chapter we have again encountered the question of whether processing is achieved in series or in parallel. Chapter 8 is devoted to a discussion of what this distinction entails and the related evidence.

8
Modes of information processing

Serial or parallel processing

We have bumped into one question repeatedly in the last four chapters without stopping to consider what form the answer to it might take. This is the question of whether processing involves handling one item at a time (serial processing) or several items at once (parallel processing) (also see A5). In Chapter 4, in our first encounter with a theory of pattern recognition, we met Noton and Stark's (1971) suggestion that recognition is achieved by serial reconstruction based on a collection of salient features. In contrast, Selfridge's (1959) Pandemonium model asserted that recognition involves the operation of a parallel bank of feature analysers. The serial-parallel issue also figured in the discussion of visual information storage, where the nature of the transfer from VIS to later storage systems was in question. Finally, the distinction was also seen in the development from the serial, switching filter model of attention proposed by Broadbent (1958), to the parallel, selective attenuation model of Treisman (1964b), in which the processing of many sources of information can be carried on simultaneously.

We will pause, therefore, to take a closer look at the question, and the evidence relating to it. Given that the ball was set rolling in the previous chapter it seems appropriate to do so in the context of the visual processing of characters.

Multiple-target tasks

There are some signs that we can achieve parallel processing. Silent reading, for example, can proceed at such a rate (up to 1,000 words per minute) that letter-by-letter processing seems most unlikely. But we should be wary of this kind of example since it may simply indicate the importance of factors like context (Ch. 9). We had better rely on experimental enquiry to give us an answer to the serial-parallel question.

One experimental paradigm that was used for this purpose was described by Neisser (1963). The task was to locate and report a 'target' item embedded in a vertical column of background items ('non-targets') (see A9). Two examples of this kind are shown in Figure 8.1.

(a) Searching for the item containing Z (after Neisser, 1963)	(b) Searching for the 'different' item (10 in this case)
IVMXWE	11
WMXIEV	00
EVXMIW	00
WVEIXM	00
MIWXVE	11
IXMVEW	00
XMVZIE	11
VEWMXI	11
XWEIMV	10
IMEVWX	00

Fig. 8.1 *Examples of Neisser visual search task*

Typically a much longer list than these is presented and the subject is asked to scan systematically through it (generally he is instructed to begin at the top of the list). His time to find the target, his search time, is found to increase by a more or less constant amount for each non-target that has to be scanned before reaching the target. Therefore if the search times are plotted graphically as a function of the number of non-targets prior to the target, then they should fall on a straight line like that in Figure 8.2.

The slope of this straight line is interpreted as the scanning time for a *non-target* item. In one of Neisser's experiments the subjects, with little or no practice, scanned one six-letter row every 230 ms if searching for a Z in a list like that of Figure 8.1(a), but they attained scanning times of 75 ms per item if Q was the target in the same kind of background (the significance of the target-background relation was discussed in Chapter 7). So in the first case about four rows were scanned every second while in the second the scanning rate was in excess of thirteen rows per second (about eighty letters per second). In the second task, Figure 8.1(b), we found

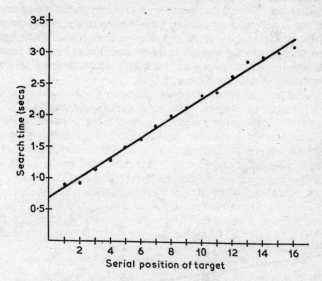

Fig. 8.2 *Example of search times obtained for an experiment using lists like those in Fig. 8.1(b)*

The straight line was fitted to the data by the 'method of least squares'. The scanning rate is 160 ms per item.

scanning times between 70 and 160 ms per item. Scanning times for word targets in word search lists are of the same order: Neisser and Beller (1965) obtained values in the region of 175 ms per word (about 6 per second) when the target was a proper name or the name of an animal.

Another of Neisser's findings was that searching for two alternative targets (e.g. H or Z) was, with a good deal of practice, no faster than searching for four alternatives (e.g. H, M, Q or Z). In a follow-up to this, Neisser, Novick and Lazar (1963) found that scanning times converged with practice to become virtually equal whether the subject searched for one, five or even ten alternative targets, although there were large differences in the scanning times at the outset. Their subjects worked for over twenty days at this task and comparable acts of heroism have been demonstrated in similar studies. Neisser and his colleagues concluded that given sufficient practice parallel processing of up to ten targets could be achieved.

Further research has been done to determine whether this effect is achieved by trading speed for accuracy; conclusions from these studies are much less sanguine about whether parallel processing can be attained since accuracy does tend to fall (i.e. more targets are missed) if scanning times are to converge (e.g. Kristofferson, 1972).

Another experimental paradigm widely adopted for the purpose of investigating the serial-parallel question was introduced by Sternberg (1966). A set of 'target' characters (no more than six in number, usually letters or digits) is shown for a matter of seconds for the subject to memorize. He is then shown a single 'probe' or 'test' character and has to make a response indicating whether the probe is one of the memory set. Sternberg found that for every character added to the memory set, reaction time (RT) increased by about 35–40 ms, i.e. RT was a linear function of the size of the memory set. It can be inferred from this that the probe is compared with each target character in turn; processing is serial.

A surprising result was that the rate of increase was the same whether there was a match (positive response) or no match (negative response) between the probe and one of the memory set. It is surprising because this result seems to show that the comparison process is not just serial but *exhaustive* – that it continues right through the memory set even when a match between the probe and a target has been found. A more intuitively plausible situation would be for the comparison to be self-terminating, in the sense that it ceases as soon as a match occurs (Sternberg, 1975, observed that the intuitions of computer engineers are not offended by the concept of exhaustive processing). If the search were self-terminating upon success, the positive response could be made when, on average, half the memory set had been processed, while the negative response would necessarily be held back until all possible targets had been checked against the probe. The slope of the negative RT function ought to have been twice that of the positive RT function. So the conclusion seems to be that memory comparison is serial and exhaustive.

But things are never so straightforward as this, and if we doctor the parallel processing assumption in the same way, making use of the self-terminating vs. exhaustiveness distinction, then it is possible to devise a parallel model which also predicts a very similar outcome.

On the face of it a parallel model predicts that RT should be independent of the size of the memory set, and this is indeed the case if processing is self-terminating or if the processing times are always the same. Since all psychological processes seem to involve variability (often to an embarrassing degree as far as psychologists are concerned), the assumption of fixed processing times does not seem plausible. But if processing is not simply parallel but exhaustive as well, then RT increases with set size. To see this suppose we have a roomful of people and the height of the tallest of them is noted. For a larger collection of people, then although the average height will remain more or less the same (assuming the same basic population is drawn on), the range of heights is likely to increase. There is more chance of finding extremely tall or extremely short people in the larger sample. So, concentrating on one aspect, the height of the tallest person in the room will tend to increase as the number of people increases. If we liken the Sternberg targets to the people, and the processing times to their heights, then the outcome of exhaustive parallel processing is analogous to the measurement of maximum height; thus RT will increase with set size.

In fact this modification cannot by itself account for the linear relation between RT and set size. It turns out that RT certainly increases, but not necessarily in a linear fashion. Yet other assumptions are needed for this purpose, for example, relating to the statistical properties of the processes involved. Nevertheless, this serves to show that there is so much room for manoeuvre that the choice of a model is very difficult.

A parallel model which does predict the linear relation assumes that processing capacity is fixed (Ch. 6). Initially this fixed capacity is evenly distributed over all target alternatives simultaneously, and it is evenly redistributed over the remaining alternatives whenever the processing of one of them is completed. Eventually only one remains and this receives the benefit of the total processing capacity for the rest of the time. This brings to light an assumption that has been lurking beneath the surface of the previous discussion, that the processing time of one item is unrelated to that of another. In this *capacity distribution* model the assumption of independence is relaxed.

The importance of this is the revelation of a whole collection of assumptions and options that are involved even in the confines of simple problems like these. There are two fundamental dichotomies between serial and parallel processing, and between exhaustive and self-terminating methods. Other distinctions made in this discussion include that between fixed and variable processing times, and lastly that between related and unrelated processing times. The problem of the identifiability of serial and parallel models (i.e. the difficulty of telling one apart from the other) has been discussed by Townsend (1971). Although there is a bewildering range of alternatives, theory builders tend, not unreasonably, to work with a fairly limited range of models. We shall do the same.

Tidy conclusions are therefore not possible, but if we take a consensus view it would probably be that Neisser's results favour something very close to a parallel self-terminating process while Sternberg's support a serial exhaustive process. This discrepancy in itself is untidy, and has yet to be adequately explained.

Multi-attribute stimulus classification

Another task that is popular among investigators of the serial-parallel question is where the subject has to judge whether a pair of stimuli are the same or different. What is of interest is whether the time to make the judgement depends on the number of 'attributes' or 'dimensions' on which the stimuli vary. Attributes that have been used for this purpose include size, shape, colour and brightness.

Egeth (1966) found that when stimuli are different the RT decreases as the number of attribute differences increases. This suggests that attributes are compared one after another and the response is made as soon as a discrepancy is discovered on any attribute; this is serial self-terminating processing. But this would also predict that when there are no differences to detect (i.e. the stimuli are the same) the RT should be slowest of all because all attributes have to be checked. The kind of data obtained in this sort of experiment is illustrated in Figure 8.3; the 'same' RT has an intermediate position relative to the 'different' RTs as indicated by the arrows.

What are we to make of this anomaly? After all, it is a fairly minor irregularity and it might seem a little excessive to send up a shout of alarm. However, it meshes in with a collection of like findings (discussed presently) which could

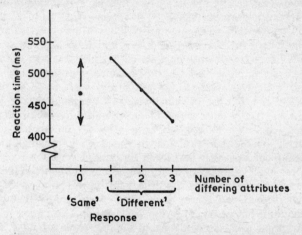

Fig. 8.3 *Typical findings when reaction time to two stimuli is plotted against the number of attributes on which the stimuli differ*

foreshadow the need to make some fundamental qualifications of the serial-parallel assumptions.

Wholes and parts

It is one of the canons of perception psychology that 'the whole is different from the sum of its parts'. The essence of this view is that the perception of an object or event cannot be predicted accurately from a knowledge of the perceptions of the elementary parts of the object or event. This 'wholistic' hypothesis is one of the important contributions of Gestalt psychology:

The way in which parts are seen, in which subwholes

109

emerge, in which grouping occurs, is not an arbitrary piece-meal ... summation of elements, but is a process in which characteristics of the whole play a major determining role. (Wertheimer, 1958, p. 135)

Gestalt theory also embodied a wholistic approach to the perceptual *system*, which was considered to be organized as a whole, on an instantaneous basis. Accordingly, it would follow that an attempt to analyse the perceptual system into component processes would be ill-conceived.

The Gestalt viewpoint provided a fruitful conceptual atmosphere for thinking about perception, but at the same time imposed its own limitations on possible lines of enquiry since some of its assumptions attained the status of un-spoken dogmas. During the past fifteen years or so a good deal of research has been motivated by questions that repre-sent an equally quiet denial of the wholistic hypothesis. The chief challenge to the wholistic view is represented im-plicitly by the analytical models based on information-pro-cessing concepts that have been introduced since Chapter 5. These kinds of models would have been out of court so far as Gestalt psychology was concerned. But in this short space of time method and theory have evolved so rapidly that the pendulum has begun to swing back again. The notion of a perceptual response being based on the whole stimulus, on the global aspect it presents, is again being discussed. For someone trained to think of stimuli analytically it may be hard to grasp what the wholistic hypothesis entails. Neverthe-less it seems to provide a useful alternative perspective from which to view some of the research in this chapter.

Beyond serial and parallel processing

Some of the difficulties facing a theoretical approach which takes the serial-parallel dichotomy as one of its cornerstones were explained by Marcel (1970) in the course of an investi-gation using multi-attribute stimuli. In his experiment Marcel used four stimulus attributes: background colour (red or green), shape (circle or square), orientation of a bar drawn across the shape (vertically or horizontally) and the continuity of the bar (solid or broken). The subject had to make one re-sponse to a 'positive' stimulus, and another response to a 'negative' one. A positive stimulus was defined in terms of particular combinations of two attributes, e.g. red and square, vertical and broken bar, etc. A negative stimulus was defined as all others.

In one condition the attribute combinations were themselves combined disjunctively. Thus the positive stimulus might be defined as '*either* red and square *or* vertical and broken bar'. In this condition reaction times to negative stimuli were systematically longer than those to positive ones. An interesting conclusion was reached by considering the number of attributes that a subject would have to examine before he could make a response in the two cases. The positive RTs were always faster, even when the number of attributes needed for a response was effectively the same as the number needed for a negative response. In contrast the number of attribute *combinations* needed for a positive response was always less than for a negative response. Marcel, therefore, concluded that it was the attribute combination that was used in testing a stimulus, not the attributes taken singly. So the subject had adopted a kind of superordinate attribute in which, for example, redness and squareness were submerged. Marcel described these as *functional attributes*.

The stimulus attributes in this experiment were of a fairly obvious kind. A case could be made, however, for considering other stimuli in the same way. For example, letters can be thought of as consisting of aspects, features or attributes like curvedness, angularity, closedness, tailedness, etc. Marcel (1970) made just this point and suggested that such stimuli could potentially be processed just like the more obvious kinds of multi-attribute stimuli. Marcel's experiment tells us little that is directly relevant to character recognition, although it demonstrates the importance of knowing what are the functional attributes used by the subject.

Blobs

A related but much simpler experiment by Biederman and Checkosky (1970) showed that rather quicker discrimination between two stimuli was achieved if they varied in both size and brightness as opposed to size or brightness only. This suggests a horse-race model in which the 'winner' is the 'horse' (attribute) which gets processed first. This is a parallel self-terminating model (it is as if in the example on page 107 we were looking for the shortest person in the room).

In this experiment either attribute could be used to discriminate between the stimuli because the values were *correlated* or *redundant*. Thus the brightest stimulus was also the largest one, and the dimmest was the smallest. What would happen if brightness and size were not correlated, i.e. if they varied *orthogonally*? Garner and Felfoldy (1970) have done this experiment, although with other stimulus attributes. They also found an improvement in speed of discrimination when attributes were combined in a correlated way, but an impairment when combined orthogonally.

In addition Garner and Felfoldy found these effects disappeared if the two attributes were presented separately (as if in the Biederman and Checkosky experiment there was a size stimulus and a brightness stimulus side by side). They discussed their findings in terms of the *integrality* versus *separability* of the attributes involved. Some background has to be filled in to explain these concepts.

In an absolute judgement task the subject is asked to identify stimuli which vary on a single attribute like size, hue or brightness. Typically they can do this accurately for around five to seven stimuli. Not surprisingly they do better if the stimuli vary on two or more dimensions at a time. For example, in an experiment in which tones varying on six different attributes (loudness, pitch, duration and so on) were used, Pollack and Ficks (1954) found that more than 200 tones could be identified. A more intriguing finding for our purposes, however, is that by Eriksen and Hake, who in 1955 found that subjects could identify more than sixteen stimuli (varying in size, brightness and hue) even though the values of the three attributes were perfectly correlated with one another. This was a considerable improvement over the performance with the single attributes.

Lockhead (1966) replicated this latter finding for stimuli varying in hue and brightness, but showed further that if the two values for any stimulus were presented in different locations on the same card there was no gain from redundancy, and no loss due to orthogonality. Lockhead went on to introduce the concepts of integrality and separability. An integral stimulus is one on whose attributes the subject operates together. A non-integral or separable stimulus is one in which the information about each attribute can be handled independently of the other. The distinction seems to be whether or not the attributes can be psychologically separated in an analogous fashion to the physical separation used by the experimenters.

As Lockhead admitted, this is not a very clear conceptual distinction; the integral stimulus is exemplified, he suggested, by a Christmas tree! 'We perceive its size, brightness, hue and shape together, and it is difficult to perceive one of these aspects without the others' (Lockhead, 1972, p. 411). Of course it is *possible* to perceive the aspects separately, but it is difficult. This is an appealing example but it might be more helpful for us to take the human face, or the printed or written word, as the paradigm of an integral stimulus. Lockhead in fact *defined* integral attributes as those for which discrimination is facilitated when the attributes are correlated and impaired when orthogonal.

He went on to argue that integral stimuli are processed as entities and that their constituent values are not ordinarily assessed or analysed unless the task demands it. The evidence actually seems to contradict the idea that the values are not analysed, since it is not clear how else the gains and losses from redundancy and orthogonality could come about. It clearly depends on what is meant by 'analysis' and it may be better for us to conceptualize integral attributes as those which are perceptually not capable of being 'pulled apart'.

One feature of most studies in which attribute-redundancy has been investigated is that the correlation of values on two or more attributes is linear. Thus the pairing of values to produce two-attribute stimuli will generally involve taking the largest value on one attribute with the largest value on the second attribute. Figure 8.4 shows an example of this. It may help to think of A as size and B as brightness, although it is not clear whether these are integral attributes (the evidence of Biederman and Checkosky, 1970 confirmed the redundancy gain property, but the orthogonality interference property does not seem to have been demonstrated yet). The stimuli used in the experiment would be those represented by the Xs on the diagonal of the square. But this is not a mandatory arrangement and a different way of combining the values could be used, such as that shown by the Os in Figure 8.5.

This combination of attribute values is called the sawtooth pairing (the dotted lines, which should otherwise be ignored, will explain why). The second attribute is still redundant and so the question about the effects of redundancy could be asked about this situation too. The crucial question is whether discrimination among the four stimuli in the X set is as easy as among the four in the O set.

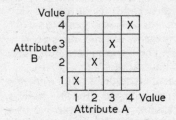

Fig. 8.4 *Linear combination of attribute values*

The experiment has been done, and although the result was not too clear it suggested that the O set was responded to *faster* than the X set. Lockhead (1972) pointed out that the horse-race or parallel self-terminating model, which nicely accounted for the findings of Biederman and Checkosky, has some difficulty with this result, because the duration of the race should not depend on the choice of runners in this way.

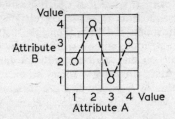

Fig. 8.5 *Sawtooth pairing of attribute values*

He therefore proposed that the stimulus is first processed wholistically – as a *'blob'*. When dealing with a given stimulus the subject first treats it as a blob and if the task demands it he then gets on with a serial analysis of the attribute values.

But how does this explain the O-set advantage? To answer this, and at the same time perhaps clarify what is a *'blob'*, we have to compare the two tasks faced by the subject in terms

114

of Figures 8.4 and 8.5. We assume that the stimuli can be represented in terms of their psychological distance from one another by means of a rectangular or matrix layout as in these figures. Lockhead suggests that the problem for the subject is to locate the stimulus in the psychological space to which it belongs without analysing the space in terms of its dimensions (attributes). This is blob processing. The advantage to the O set would follow because the distance as the crow flies between the members of the O set (join every one to every other to see this) is on average less than the distance between the members of the X set.

According to this argument (and we know of no relevant data), it would be as easy to discriminate between X-set stimuli as between stimuli constructed to have negatively correlated values (represented by the cells on the other diagonal). Are these blobs as good as one another for the purpose of discrimination?

One of the intriguing conclusions from Lockhead's reasoning is that parallel processing is not required and the results are explainable by blob processing. But he does not seem to have accounted for the redundancy and orthogonality effects with integral stimuli. The other interesting suggestion is that the relations between attributes may be processed prior to the values of the attributes.

If blob processing represents the placing of a stimulus in its psychological space without providing much in the way of detail about the position occupied by the stimulus, it might also apply to stimuli like faces, digits, letters and words. Nevertheless it is not enough for us to conclude that subjects may process stimuli as whole configurations. This really only describes a capability and falls short of explaining it.

Review

The evidence is quite equivocal so far as mode of processing is concerned: it may be serial, parallel or neither. Even with the addition of assumptions about how much information is processed before a response is initiated, some of the evidence is uncomfortable for the simple serial or parallel processing models. Performance on tasks in which a speeded judgement has to be made about some aspect of a multi-attribute stimulus or a simple pattern pose particular problems for these models.

115

The research on serial and parallel processing seems if anything to make the task of the pattern recognition theorist even harder, since it appears that the ways of processing information are more varied than was at first imagined. In certain situations, and usually with the benefit of practice, a person may come to respond to the stimulus in some kind of global fashion based on the overall configuration it presents rather than in terms of its components, or the sum of them. It is possible that this wholistic method of processing represents the way in which highly familiar stimuli are dealt with. It is therefore of interest that Clifton (1973) found that the size of the target set in the Sternberg paradigm made no difference to RT when the target alternatives were the names of the subject's relatives and friends. The concept of a 'blob' seems to lack something in the way of a technical aura even if it has a respectable pedigree from Gestalt psychology. However, given the evidence, something of the sort seems to be necessary for a complete explanation of pattern recognition.

9
Expectations and context

If we have to allow for the gannet-like approach of blob processing then we also have to take account of the more reflective style of processing implied by the effects of context and expectations. Some evidence was presented in Chapter 6 that information selection is made easier if there is a semantic thread for the selectional system to follow. In Chapters 7 and 8 we concentrated for the most part on situations where stimuli could be considered in isolation from one another, so there was no message-as-a-whole to exert any effect. Speech recognition was an exception to this although we have yet to discuss it in these terms.

Analysis-by-synthesis

The theories of pattern recognition outlined in Chapter 7 are little more than programmatic – they suggest the kinds of explanatory concepts that may be useful but are rather weak in terms of clear-cut prediction. For example, feature analysis theories do little more than suggest that 'features' should turn out to be important empirically. Some kind of elaboration of the theory seems to be necessary.

We begin with the motor theory of speech recognition. In its crudest form this theory maintains that we recognize speech by generating movements in the articulatory system. The signal produced by these movements is checked against the speech signal, and the movements are modified if there is a mismatch. These processes of generating a signal and checking it are repeated until an acceptable signal is produced; when this happens the speech signal has been 'recognized'. One of the drawbacks of this theory is the sheer number of matches needed to recognize anything drawn from a large 'vocabulary' of signals. Another consideration is that the generated signal cannot be an audible one since we do not repeat aloud what we are listening to, although lip movements are sometimes made by old people when following a conversation. The generation process needs to be made less haphazard and to be silent!

One approach to the silent signal problem is to distinguish between the programming of the articulatory system for action, and the action itself. The generated signal could correspond to the mere setting-up of the programme for action (as if shaping-up to speak but making no sound). Even this may be an unreasonable assumption since speech can be understood in the absence of the ability to articulate (Lenneberg, 1962), and children understand speech before being able to talk themselves. However, the notion is that in some sense we hear speech by producing it, at some level, internally.

Since the generated signal is formed from some lower order entities, like phonemes or articulatory movements, the process can be described as analysing the signal by synthesis. The analysis-by-synthesis approach may in addition accommodate the problem of dealing with a large number of alternative signals, by assuming that there is some preliminary analysis used to limit the number of internal signals that need to be generated. An economy of this sort is usually thought to be necessary.

The motor theory could presumably be applied direct to visual pattern recognition, but this is not generally supported. However, the evidence that recognition is facilitated by eye movements (Noton and Stark, 1971) suggests a plausible way of translating the theory. Nevertheless, an extreme form of the theory would be hard to maintain, not least because an eye-movement by itself signals very little about the visual world. There is, therefore, some difficulty in generalizing this approach to visual perception because of the difficulty of conceiving what might be constructed and what the precise analogues of articulatory movements might be.

One advocate of the 'constructive' approach to visual perception was Neisser (1967). He argued that the resources of the perceptual system can be allocated in one of two ways. First, they may be applied to the visual scene in a global wholistic fashion to provide information about the presence of objects and to segregate them into figural entities. Beyond this they supply data to guide later processes. This basic mode of operation was called *pre-attentive analysis*. Besides the guidance of more sophisticated processing mechanisms, Neisser supposed that pre-attentive control was exercised over everyday activities like walking, and visually 'tracking' moving objects, tasks which seem to require relatively little attention to detail.

This contrasts with the analysis carried out using '*focal attention*', which is considered to follow on from, and capitalize on, the global segregative activities of pre-attentive analysis. Neisser bracketed this conception with that of figural synthesis. By this means he emphasized the constructive nature of the operations of focal attention: 'one does not simply examine the input and make a decision; one *builds* an appropriate visual object'. Because focal attention involved the detailed scrutiny of the stimulus, Neisser supposed that this was carried out on a *serial* basis, in contrast to the free-wheeling *parallel* activity of pre-attentive analysis. He thus concluded that his own visual search experiments, with their evidence of parallel processing, were carried out pre-attentively. On the other hand, situations like that of the Sternberg paradigm (see p. 106), in which close scrutiny of a single stimulus is needed, were dealt with by serial processing in focal attention.

There are, therefore, theoretical precedents for supposing that perceptual processing involves a preliminary stage at which global characteristics of the input are extracted. The kind of information available at this stage is probably of a low order (hue, size, brightness). However, in view of Beck's (1966) findings on perceptual segregation, features like line tilt may be very quickly available, and it would be as well not to underestimate the capabilities at this 'primitive' level. But if the input has to be analysed in detail it may be necessary to construct a representation of it by a process like that of figural synthesis. The raw material for this purpose is presumably the feature information supplied by the preliminary analysis, supplemented by information extracted once attention has been focused, but exactly what is constructed in figural synthesis remains vague. More critically, it is not clear *how* the 'visual object' is put together.

Perceptual hypotheses

A well-known view of perception as a constructive enterprise is expressed by Gregory (1966): '... perception involves going beyond the immediately given evidence of the senses'. Moreover, 'this evidence is assessed on many grounds and generally we make the best bet, and see things more or less correctly'. If, as he maintains, 'a perceived object is a hypothesis, suggested and tested by sensory data', then the perception will be in error to the extent that the assessment of the evidence is faulty and the wrong bet made.

An example of how the wrong bet may come to be made is provided by the Ames 'distorted room' (see cover). Ames constructed a room so that when viewed from a particular point it gave rise to a retinal image like that due to an ordinary rectangular room. So in the cover picture the left-hand corner of the room is in fact much further away than the right-hand corner, and it is correspondingly expanded. It seems that the perceptual 'bet' is made that the room is indeed rectangular as can be seen by the fact that two people of the same height standing in the corners of the room look markedly different in size, and a person walking from one corner to the other appears to change size. The alternative bet, that the room is a peculiar shape, is more likely to be made if the odds are changed; if the people in the room are very familiar to the viewer, or it is a close relative who walks across the room, then the odd shape of the room is more likely to be seen.

The visual illusions of Figure 9.1 also demonstrate how the perceptual system may be misled. They have long intrigued perception psychologists and a great deal of theoretical effort has been devoted to explaining how they come about. In the context of a constructive theory like Gregory's the task is to establish the evidence on which the perceptual system bases its hypotheses.

We may begin with the observation that illusion figures can sometimes be construed as simple perspective drawings of aspects of three-dimensional objects. The Müller-Lyer illusion with the outgoing fins can be thought of as the inside corner of a room (or box), and the figure with the ingoing fins as the outside corner of a building (or box) (Fig. 9.2).

One early theory in fact maintained that perspective information suggests depth and by so doing produces changes in the apparent size of certain parts of the figure. If the retinal image includes a pair of converging lines then they are quite

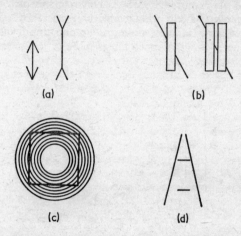

Fig. 9.1 *Set of four optico-geometric illusions*

(a) Müller-Lyer: the shafts of the arrows are the same length.
(b) Poggendorf: the diagonals are interrupted straight lines.
(c) Woodworth: the square is true.
(d) Ponzo: otherwise called the 'railway track' illusion; the two short lines are the same length.

likely to arise from lines 'out there' which in fact are extended in space. So the fins in the left-hand arrowheads in Figure 9.1(a) would represent lines receding from the vertical shaft, and the fins in the right-hand figure would stand for lines approaching us from the shaft. Thus the shaft on the left is nearer to us than that on the right. But since they cast retinal images of the same size, if the left-hand shaft is to be nearer, we reason that it must also be the smaller of the two. The same kind of argument can be applied to the Ponzo illusion in Figure 9.1(d).

There seems to be some sleight of word in this explanation and the reader may be uncertain of some of the steps in the argument. This uncertainty is quite common, and indeed Gregory (1966) argued that perspective theory made just the opposite prediction to the one we have just produced from it! Gregory's solution was not to abandon perspective theory altogether but to retain the suggestion that depth information is somehow available and to capitalize on the explanatory potential of *size constancy scaling*. This refers to the remarkable perceptual process whereby an object is seen as much the same size at different distances despite drastic changes

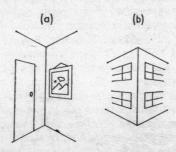

Fig. 9.2 *'Ecological' version of the Müller-Lyer illusion figures (after Gregory, 1966)*

in the size of the image it casts on the retina. Other constancy mechanisms enable us to allow for physical changes in the illumination and shape of stimuli. The size of the retinal image halves every time the distance between object and observer doubles. But should a man who is 6 feet tall walk from a point 10 feet distant to a second point 20 feet away, he does not appear to decrease in size, let alone shrink by 50 per cent.

Size constancy scaling can be seen in action by viewing a clear after-image, of something like a photographic flash, projected onto surfaces at different distances. The after-image will increase dramatically in size as one's gaze is directed from a nearby surface to a much more distant one. This indicates that apparent distance may be important in the determination of apparent size; the precise relation between them is known as Emmert's law.

The importance of all this is that size constancy demonstrates a means whereby a compensatory perceptual adjustment is habitually achieved, though it could in principle misfire. While it is an adaptive process in most circumstances the 'compensation' would turn out to be a 'distortion' if it were triggered inappropriately – say, by the perspective information in a flat figure.

It has to be explained why the perspective information does not lead the flat figures to look other than flat. Gregory argued that this is because they are seen as lying in a flat surface, and he demonstrated that they take on a three-dimensional appearance if they are presented in the form of luminous two-dimensional outlines in the dark. In the absence of the textured appearance of the paper on which they are drawn, they spontaneously acquire the looks of inside and outside corners as predicted. However, this has been found hard to replicate by Hotopf (1966), among others.

Gregory assumed that constancy scaling could be brought into action by depth cues that are otherwise ineffective in producing apparent distance in the figures and tested this by measuring the apparent depth of one of the luminous illusion figures. They were indeed found to have apparent depth and the amount varied as the amount of distortion changed (this was induced by using different arrowhead angles). However, it has been observed that instead of the distortion of the shafts of the Müller-Lyer figure being due to the perspective information supplied by the fins, it is as valid to claim, on the same evidence, the reverse, viz. that the apparent perspective of the fins and any apparent depth effects are a consequence of the distortion (Stacey and Pike, 1970).

If constancy scaling can be thought of as a constructive program for normalizing the input (like pre-processing) then attempts to disrupt its operation may throw some interesting light on the details of the program. For our purposes, however, the theory is important in emphasizing the constructive nature of perception and its dependence on expectation. In particular, Gregory's theory illustrates how perceptual error could arise when expectations are not confirmed. Expectations depend partly upon a context. In this case there were contextual data of an irrelevant kind (i.e. supplied by the arrowheads) and these were allegedly responsible for misdirecting the perceptual hypothesis generator.

Disconfirming expectations

The effect of contradicting an expectation was investigated in a quite different situation by Bruner and Postman in 1949. The subjects in their experiment were led to expect conventional playing cards but were also shown incongruous displays consisting, for example, of cards with black hearts or red spades. Recognition of the incongruous cards occurred at longer exposures than for normal cards. This in itself is not surprising if we think in terms of *responses*, because the probability of calling something like the 'black four of hearts' must be rather low. The interesting finding that suggests a *perceptual* effect was that some subjects reported compromise perceptions of the incongruous cards. They saw brown or purple hearts, or cards in black with red edges.

The effects of disconfirmed expectations can be informally demonstrated with some examples from reading. Further down in the text are a couple of sentences that the reader should avoid looking at for the time being. They are prefaced by a pair of asterisks, and care should be taken to fixate steadily on the asterisks before starting to read, preferably aloud. The first sentence follows immediately below:

**The cat sat on the map and licked its whiskers.

In this case the expectation for the word 'mat' was hopefully produced by the very familiar sequence at the beginning of the sentence. Some readers may have found themselves doing a 'double-take' in order to read it. Now do exactly the same thing for the next sentence:

**The cat sat on the mantelpiece and licked its whiskers.

The expectation for 'mat' is again disconfirmed. Admittedly it has probably been revised as a result of the previous experience, so this is not a very pure demonstration.

Naturally we should want to put this demonstration on a formal basis. It is instructive to consider how this could be done; the difficulties of measuring the effect and of dissuading the subject from 'seeing through' the experiment are the chief stumbling-blocks. The former could perhaps be overcome by measuring the time to begin speaking the sentences (a 'control' sentence with 'mat' in its rightful place would need to be used). But the problem of not making the experiment transparent to the subject is a particularly thorny one. A solution would be to prepare many sentences of this sort and to ask each subject to read only one of them (preceded by some experience with unexceptional sentences). It is also a useful exercise to consider what effects on eye movement would be expected. Of course, if eye movements were recorded and only a single critical datum were obtained there would be serious grounds for questioning the economics of the experiment.

In the first example it is likely that the fovea has to be more or less directly aimed at the word 'map' before its incongruity in the context is noticed. Incongruity seems to be signalled earlier in the second case, presumably on account of the more obviously discrepant word shapes of 'mantelpiece' and the expected 'mat'. Of course, the effect must be reliably produced under experimental conditions before we can attach any significance to it. Nevertheless, we shall indulge in some speculation about it. First, it seems to demonstrate the importance of word shape in reading, and suggests that this kind of information can be signalled via the periphery. This is consistent with data considered in Chapter 2. The first of the sentences seems to involve discrimination on the basis of a detailed inspection of a foveally presented stimulus; it seems to involve a contradiction of a well-advanced synthesis operation. On the other hand, the second sentence appears to receive pre-attentive analysis of peripheral visual information.

The possibility that even *semantic* attributes can be picked up extrafoveally has received some support in a recent experiment by Edwards and Goolkasian (1974). Their subjects performed well above a chance level when asked to give the name of the category to which a three-letter word belonged (animals, parts of body, etc.) even at a distance of 10 degrees from the fovea.

Expectations and instructions

A constructive theory like Neisser's has the advantage of enabling us to take context effects into account. It is easy to see how a constructive process could be biased in such a way as to reflect the individual's expectations.

Expectations may depend on recent or distant experience, including instructions, graphical and semantic context. They may serve to reduce the number of candidates for synthesis or the order in which candidates are considered. Of course, this tends to create a new set of problems since we now have to explain the machinery for doing this – for establishing the expectations and for mediating their effect on the synthesis operations. This does not preclude bias being exerted at the preliminary feature analysis stage. This could be done as in a Pandemonium system by modifying the weights or criteria attached to different features or combinations of features. A considerable amount of research has been devoted to the investigation of the kind of bias that can be produced by instructions. This is the problem of *perceptual set*; the evidence has been comprehensively reviewed by Haber (1966). One of the commonest techniques of this research is to present tachistoscopically a multi-attribute stimulus (perhaps varying in colour, size, shape and number of elements), with instructions that one of the dimensions is more important in some way. Performance on the emphasized attribute, that which the subject was 'set' for, is of course of central interest. The question is whether the selectivity implied by the instructions leads to a clearer perception of the emphasized attribute.

The original experiments on set simply asked the subject to pay particular attention to one attribute, but otherwise to report all the details of the display. So he might be told to concentrate on the colours of the objects, and better performance on colour would be interpreted as showing enhanced perception. But this experiment confounds perception and memory. The poorer performance on the non-emphasized attributes could simply result from their being more affected by decay of the icon, or being less efficiently stored.

Recognition of this shortcoming led to the introduction of the before-versus-after procedure, in which the effect of set given in advance of stimulus presentation is compared with set given after the display. The results seemed to settle the question in favour of the perception hypothesis, since the advantage to the emphasized attribute tended to be lost when the instruction was delayed until after the stimulus. But this experimental paradigm is not entirely satisfactory either, since it can be argued that the advantage when the instructions are given before the display is due to a quicker, more efficient storage of the emphasized attribute. More specifically, it has been claimed that the effect of set is tied up with the order of reporting attributes, and the differential opportunity for rehearsal of the emphasized attribute.

A popular view is that it is the order in which the attributes are *encoded* from the icon that is crucial. Harris and Haber (1963) reported an experiment in which two encoding strategies were used. In the first strategy the subject was instructed to report the display by an objects code (e.g. 'two blue squares, three red circles'); this was compared with a strategy in which the subject was asked to use a dimensions code, in which the values on each attribute were reported together (e.g. 'two, three; blue, red; squares, circles'). Performance of the dimensions coders was much better on the emphasized attributes, but there was no advantage of emphasis for the objects coders. This seems to imply that the subjects using the dimensions code encoded the attributes flexibly, reflecting the instructions about which attribute to emphasize. Nevertheless, the objects coders were more proficient, perhaps indicating that this more familiar code, which is consistent with English syntax, leads to faster encoding.

Not all the evidence on set favours an explanation based on non-perceptual factors. Long, Reid and Henneman (1960), in one of a series of studies, described some simple procedures that gave evidence of an effect on perception. In one case one of two letters was displayed and the subject was told the two alternatives before or after presentation. The before condition gave better performance than the after condition. In another experiment a pair of degraded letters was presented and he was asked to say which of them was a given target letter. Giving the target in advance led to better discrimination performance than delaying it. Both these findings suggest that perceptual bias can be obtained.

Egeth and Smith (1967) presented pictures as the response alternatives because they were dissatisfied with some earlier work in which category names were used as the alternatives. They reasoned that using verbal labels might prevent the subject from knowing in advance what the critical distinctive features might be. In this experiment, being given an advance view of the response alternatives proved to be an advantage over when they were only seen after the display. This by itself suggests a perceptual effect. Egeth and Smith also compared similar alternatives (e.g. four different shoes) with dissimilar alternatives (e.g. shoe, motorcycle, radio, vacuum cleaner). The difference between these conditions was reduced when the alternatives were previewed, which reinforces the conclusion that the perceptual system can be tuned to extract salient information to aid discrimination.

Gummerman (1971) adopted a methodological improvement also introduced by Egeth and Smith. This is to present the alternatives before *and* after the display and to compare this with an after-only condition. The rationale for this is that in the usual before-only condition, by the time he gets tested the subject may have forgotten where the response alternatives were. Gummerman showed one of a set of stimuli (four or sixteen in number) and two alternative stimuli were also shown. Previewing gave no advantage if the response alternatives were drawn from among four stimuli. There was, however, a sizeable drop in performance for the after-only condition when the response alternatives were two from sixteen stimuli. Gummerman concluded that selective perception is possible but only when 'foreknowledge significantly reduces the size of the effective stimulus set'.

The effect of set on the perceptual system, therefore, seems to be limited to situations where the number of options for the analysis-by-synthesis operation can be *effectively* reduced. In simpler situations, like those of Long *et al.*, (1960), it is conceivable that the effect is obtained through biased information extraction in the Pandemonium system. The encoding effects may be mediated by a bias on the order of operations in analysis-by-synthesis. This, of course, does not preclude other memory or response effects. The research on perceptual set represents one aspect of the general problem of selective attention (Chs. 5 and 6). The experiments in these areas have a number of operational similarities, but the main resemblance is a theoretical one, namely the question of whether or not perceptual selectivity is indeed perceptual, or is a result of selective memory or responding.

Reading between the lines
An important point that seems to emerge from the discussions of the constructive theorists is that attention is not distinct but an aspect of perception. 'Attention' describes the selectional characteristics of perception. Contextual variables supply one way of guiding these selective processes. In reading text or listening to speech the message as a whole provides a cognitive 'target' for the individual to 'track'.

In both cases we make use of the large 'redundancy' of the

English language (see A7) to find our way about the message. For example, the text we are reading may be mutilated in various ways, from damage to or removal of single characters, to the removal of whole words. And yet we understand the material without much hesitation or difficulty, and may even pass one of these 'errors' without noticing it. Although in one sense this denotes a lack of precision on the part of the pattern recognition system, surely it ought to be considered as an example of the flexibility of the total processing system; in any case, the fallacy of supposing that this represents some kind of perceptual error is demonstrated by the fact that the same system can be 'tuned' to search for these same typographical errors (proof-readers do this professionally).

The central role of expectancies (expectations) in perceiving and attending has been re-emphasized by Hochberg (1970). In the particular case of reading, Hochberg asserted that the task for the reader '... is to fixate only those parts of the visual array that (he) expects (on the basis of previous semantic and syntactic constraints and on the basis of how words and spaces appear to peripheral vision) and which will enable him to check his guesses about what is being said, and will help him to formulate further anticipations' (Hochberg, 1970, p. 117).

But expectations play a quite general role. They are involved also in the perception of form: 'The mature observer has a vocabulary of sequential visuomotor expectancies (e.g. "If I look along this edge to the left, I will see a corner concave to the right")' (Hochberg, 1970, p. 114). An important venture for the future, according to Hochberg, is the discovery of the vocabulary and the grammar of visual perception.

We look now at some research which seems to demonstrate the involvement of context on a smaller scale. These kinds of effects must also be accounted for.

In a word

The pre-eminence of Gestalt psychology earlier this century encouraged teachers of reading to concentrate on 'whole-word' methods of introducing children to reading. One approach emphasized the overall shapes of words and they do differ clearly in this respect. Nevertheless there is little evidence as to whether people can perceive words as wholes in this or other ways.

Among recent developments in research on word recognition was the discovery that a letter can be more easily identified if it is embedded in a word than if it is one of a string of letters forming a nonsense word (non-word). This is known as the *word superiority effect*. Why should the company which the letter is keeping matter when it is a question of its own identity that seems to be crucial for responding? The original findings of Reicher (1969) were replicated several times, so this was no statistical fluke.

The experimental literature on the word superiority effect is a little tortuous and the effect has come and gone in response to different experimental variations. We quote just one of the many studies to illustrate some of the problems encountered. This is an experiment by Juola, Leavitt and Choe (1974). Instead of using RT as the measure of performance like most other experimenters, they recorded the number of occasions on which the correct one of two alternative letters was reported for a briefly displayed four-letter word or non-word. Performance was reliably better for words (74 per cent correct) than non-words (67 per cent correct). The crucial thing in this case is not the size of the difference but its reliability.

The non-words they used were highly pronounceable but 'meaningless' (e.g. bose and rist). This is important because some experimenters have used unpronounceable letter strings for the non-words. However, it is not considered to be differences in pronounceability *per se* that matter so much as differences in orthography (i.e. spelling pattern differences). So the non-words used by Juola *et al.* would not be easily differentiated from words in terms of spelling patterns, although if they were it would still pose an intriguing problem for explanation. Juola and his colleagues concluded that 'words are more perceptible because they are represented as units in an internal lexicon'. Essentially they enjoy a perceptual advantage over non-words because they have a semantic representation in memory which non-words do not have.

Thus although a word consists of units like letters (and spelling patterns) the *functional* unit involved in perceiving a word is larger than this and could even be the word itself. The conclusion seems to be that the word and its parts are easier to identify because the word has an internal representation in the subject's memory. It remains to explain how this could work. A suggestion made by Coltheart (1972) that may be helpful is that the meaning, and other characteristics of a word (like its sound and visual properties), may be extracted at the same time. Coltheart's discussion is also useful in pointing out that it is not necessary to assume that we have to identify a word before we can have some usable information about these other characteristics.

The logic of Juola and his colleagues is hard to fault and they eliminate most of the alternative explanations. But there is a point that needs to be cleared up. They used stimuli printed in lower-case letters instead of the upper-case (capital) letters used by many others. It may be a surprise to some readers that it has been more or less normative to use upper-case print in tachistoscope experiments on word recognition. Many psychologists in this field feel increasingly uncomfortable about this, but in *this* case it is possible that some global visual information was still available from words that was not present in the non-words. The use of upper-case characters would have eliminated this source of information (indeed this is the conventional rationale for using capitals). It is just possible that the word contour gives the crucial clue about the presence or absence of a given letter a little more effectively than the contour even of a pronounceable non-word. A comparison of the word superiority effect with upper- and lower-case letters would decide this.

The Juola experiment seems to show that the difference between words and non-words can be discriminated (implicitly rather than explicitly) even when the subject can perform only moderately well at the task of identifying one of its member letters. Data from some of our ongoing research suggests that the classification of a stimulus as a word or non-word, unrecognizable by itself, can be achieved at a better-than-chance level, but only if the non-words are random letters strings and not if they are word-like in construction (like those used by Juola *et al.*). But we have asked our subjects to make an explicit discrimination between the two kinds of stimuli (which it will be noted were shown so briefly that the subjects could not recognize them!). There is evidence considered next which suggests that implicit categorization of stimuli can be achieved without the need for identification.

Category effect: classification without identification?

The idea of categorization as a fundamentally important perceptual tool has been accepted for some time (Bruner, Goodnow and Austin, 1956). The point made by Bruner *et al.* is that the perceptual system needs some means for coping with the enormous range of stimuli that it meets, and some kind of preliminary classification mechanism would serve this purpose. It is not hard to understand how this could apply to the many visual stimuli that have the name 'blue', because of their physical similarities. Likewise there are physical properties that enable us to say that the person walking ahead of us is a woman rather than a man and these may precede our being able to say that it is Sarah rather than Sally; on the other hand, 'one probably decides that an object is, say, a piece of fruit by recognizing it as, say, an orange and applying the knowledge that oranges are fruit' (Nickerson, 1973).

Nickerson went on to argue that this kind of classification procedure seems to be more appropriate for classifying digits and letters, because the physical properties that could be used to distinguish letters from digits would probably be adequate for identifying individual characters. However, it is not clear that the orange-implies-fruit instance has as much force as this since it is easy to find counter-examples of the same form. Thus it seems likely that one decides that something is an oak after recognizing it as a tree.

There is some evidence that supports Nickerson's view. For example, Dick (1971) found that naming a character was much quicker than saying which class it belonged to. On the other hand, Brand (1971) found that visual search (using a task like that of Neisser, 1963) is faster if the target is from a different *category* than the background items. Thus, if the target is a digit then search is faster if the background items are letters than if they are digits. This was confirmed by Ingling (1972) who concluded that stimuli can be encoded by category immediately and that it is not necessary to make a more complete identification. Ingling used letters and numbers carefully chosen so as not to favour one or other category because of their physical appearance (3 and B, 7 and Z), and she concluded from these findings that the category effect 'depends neither on specific features of the target nor on general physical features of the target and non-target categories'.

132

Jonides and Gleitman (1972) obtained some important evidence on the category effect by using the character O as the target in visual search. Of course O could serve as the letter O ('oh') or the digit 0 ('zero'), depending on instruction. When the subject was told to search for the letter O he scanned faster if the background consisted of digits rather than letters. Similarly, searching for the same symbol but as a digit was quicker when the context was supplied by letters. This confirms the category effect when there was no physical difference between targets and non-targets for the two tasks. All of it (or most of it) seems to add up to the fact that letters are not as a class distinctively different from digits. Jonides and Gleitman suggest that categorizing needs less data from a given stimulus than identifying does. This effect was repeated with words as stimuli by one of our students, Ann Levy, who replaced the dual-purpose character 'O' by the ambiguous word 'calf'; treating 'calf' as an animal word rather than a body-part word, search was quicker if the other items in the display were body-parts, and the converse also applied. How general this is remains to be seen.

Despite some conflicting findings, it is clear that categorization can precede identification. But to explain this it is not necessary to assume that there is a categorization process that leads to an identification process. It would be enough to assume that they are organized in parallel, and for them to be capable of operating at different rates relative to one another. If categorization is sometimes quicker than identification, and sometimes slower, then the job is to decide what is responsible for producing the differential operating rates.

Concluding perspective

Continuing reference has been made, in particular in this chapter, to the perception of language in its written and spoken form. This underlines our conviction that perception is profitably thought of as being extended in time. Moreover, it occurs in a coherent internal context of expectation and prediction. Perception *is* predictive and enactive.

The traditional single trial, tachistoscopic-style experimentation has served us well in revealing a multiplicity of factors bound up in perception, and we have only sampled them in this book. A disadvantage of this style of research is that it lifts the perceptual system out of its ecological niche, where it is served by all manner of long-range contextual aids. The contexts manipulated in traditional tasks are of an essentially artificial nature. They are commonly achieved by instructional sets and as such may inhibit and conceal the computational and predictive power of the perceptual system. Everyday perception does not take place in a vacuum, or in a straight-jacket imposed by a research psychologist. A case can be made, however, against our particular emphasis on language perception as a paradigm. It is inextricably tied up with a medium that has its own special rules, and at least in the case of reading it is a quite unnatural skill. It is interesting to speculate, however, that one of the chief tasks of perception psychology may turn out to be the discovery not just of the cues, attributes and properties of objects to which we are responsive, but the syntax and semantics connecting them. We suggest little more at this stage beyond the need to examine the perceptual system in free-running circumstances like searching, looking and listening. This is technically demanding but seems increasingly to be needed on grounds of ecological validity.

It should be understood, however, that we are not advocating a retreat from the methodology of the single glance. On the contrary, as we have shown by example in this chapter it continues to have a central role in perception psychology in answering questions and clarifying issues. What we do argue for is its supplementation by a range of methods with a degree more ecological realism. A theoretical lead has been given by Hochberg and others and a corpus of findings is beginning to accumulate. This can only bode well for the study of perception, and psychology in general.

Further Reading

Dember, W. N. (1961) *The Psychology of Perception*. New York: Holt, Rinehart and Winston. An excellent readable survey of the state-of-the-art of perception psychology written just as the information-processing approach was beginning to make its mark.

Gregory, R. L. (1966) *Eye and Brain*. London: Weidenfeld and Nicolson. A beautiful little book with lots of insights and challenges about vision.

Haber, R. N. and Hershenson, M. (1973) *The Psychology of Visual Perception*. New York: Holt, Rinehart and Winston. The state-of-the-art on visual perception from an information-processing theorist's point of view.

Held, R. and Richards, W. (1972) *Perception: Mechanisms and Models*. San Francisco and London: W. H. Freeman. A superior collection of articles from *Scientific American*. Beautifully illustrated, as one might expect, and very wide-ranging.

Kahneman, D. (1973) *Attention and Effort*. Englewood Cliffs, NJ: Prentice-Hall. More advanced text on attention and cognitive processes.

Neisser, U. (1967) *Cognitive Psychology*. New York: Appleton-Century-Crofts. Seminal, much criticized, much-quoted and always readable theoretical synthesis of perceptual and cognitive processes.

References and Name Index

The numbers in italics following each entry refer to page numbers within this book.

Alpern, M. (1971) Effector mechanisms in vision. In J. A. Kling and L. A. Riggs (eds) *Woodworth and Schlosberg's Experimental Psychology* (3rd edn). New York: Holt, Rinehart and Winston. *55*

Atkinson, R. C. and Shiffrin, R. M. (1968) Human memory: a proposed system and its control processes. In *The Psychology of Learning and Motivation: Advances in Research and Theory, Vol. II.* New York: Academic Press. *69*

Averbach, E. and Coriell, A. S. (1961) Short-term memory in vision. *Bell System Technical Journal 40*: 309–28. *73*

Barber, P. J. and Folkard, S. (1972) Reaction time under stimulus uncertainty with response certainty. *Journal of Experimental Psychology 93*: 138–42. *74*

Barlow, H. B. and Levick, W. R. (1965) The mechanisms of directionally selective units in the rabbit's retina. *Journal of Physiology 178*: 477–504. *96*

Bartz, A. E. (1962) Eye-movement latency, duration, and response time as a function of angular displacement. *Journal of Experimental Psychology 64*: 318–24. *57*

Beck, J. (1966) Effect of orientation and of shape similarity on perceptual grouping. *Perception and Psychophysics 1*: 300–2. *27, 119*

Beck, J. (1972) Similarity grouping and peripheral discriminability under uncertainty. *American Journal of Psychology 85*: 1–19. *23*

Biederman, I. and Checkosky, S. F. (1970) Processing redundant information. *Journal of Experimental Psychology 83*: 486–90. *111, 112, 113, 114*

Blakemore, C. and Nachmias, J. (1971) The orientation specificity of two visual after-effects. *Journal of Physiology 213*: 157–74. *97*

Brand, J. (1971) Classification without identification in visual search. *Quarterly Journal of Experimental Psychology 23*: 178–86. *132*

Broadbent, D. E. (1958) *Perception and Communication*. Oxford: Pergamon. *79, 80, 81, 83, 84, 103*

Bruner, J. S. and Postman, L. (1949) On the perception of incongruity: a paradigm. *Journal of Personality 18*: 206–23. *124*

Bruner, J. S., Goodnow, J. J. and Austin, G. A. (1956) *A Study of Thinking*. New York: John Wiley. *132*

Bryden, M. P. (1971) Attentional strategies and short-term memory in dichotic listening. *Cognitive Psychology 2*: 99–116. *89*

Buswell, G. T. (1922) Fundamental reading habits: a study of their development. *Education Monographs (Supplement) 21*. *58*

Campbell, F. W. and Maffei, L. (1970) Electrophysiological evidence for the existence of orientation and size detectors in the human visual system. *Journal of Physiology 207*: 635–52. *98*

Cherry, E. C. (1953) Some experiments on the recognition of speech, with one and two ears. *Journal of the Acoustical Society of America 25*: 975–9. *77, 84*

Clark, W. R. and Goodman, J. S. (1974) Effects of suggestion on *d'* and *Cx* for pain detection and pain tolerance. *Journal of Abnormal Psychology 83*: 364–72. *47*

Clifton, C. (1973) Must overlearned lists be scanned? *Memory and Cognition 1*: 121–3. *116*

Coltheart, M. (1972) Visual information-processing. In P. C. Dodwell (ed.) *New Horizons in Psychology 2*. Harmondsworth: Penguin. *70, 71, 74, 131*

Coltheart, M. (1975) Iconic memory: a reply to Professor Holding. *Memory and Cognition 3*: 42–8. *72, 73*

Dale, H. C. A. (1964) Factors affecting the choice of strategy in searching. *Ergonomics 7*: 73–82. *65*

Dearborn, W. F. (1906) The psychology of reading. *Archives of Philosophy, Psychology and Scientific Methods 4*. *60*

Deutsch, J. A. and Deutsch, D. (1963) Attention: some thoretical considerations. *Psychological Review 70*: 80–90. *85, 86, 87*

Dick, A. O. (1971) Processing time for naming and categorization of letters and numbers. *Perception and Psychophysics* 9: 350–2. *132*

Dixon, N. F. (1971) *Subliminal Perception: The Nature of a Controversy*. London: McGraw-Hill. *44*

Edwards, D. C. and Goolkasian, P. A. (1974) Peripheral vision location and kinds of complex processing. *Journal of Experimental Psychology* 102: 244–9. *125*

Egeth, H. E. (1966) Parallel vs serial processes in multi-dimensional stimulus classification. *Perception and Psychophysics* 1: 245–52. *108*

Egeth, H. E. and Smith, E. E. (1967) Perceptual selectivity in a visual recognition task. *Journal of Experimental Psychology* 74: 543–9. *127, 128*

Eriksen, C. W. and Collins, J. F. (1967) Some temporal characteristics of visual pattern perception. *Journal of Experimental Psychology* 74: 476–84. *69*

Eriksen, C. W. and Hake, H. W. (1955) Multidimensional stimulus difference and accuracy of discrimination. *Journal of Experimental Psychology* 50: 153–60. *112*

Fechner, G. T. (1860) *Elemente der Psycophysik*. Leipzig: Breitkopf and Hartel. English edn 1966, *Elements of Psychophysics*, trans. by H. Adler. New York: Holt, Rinehart and Winston. *48*

Garner, W. R. and Felfoldy, G. L. (1970) Integrality of stimulus dimensions in various types of information processing. *Cognitive Psychology* 1: 225–41. *112*

Gelb, A. (1929) Farbenkonstanz der Sehdinge. *Handbuch der Normalen und Pathologischen Physiologie* 12: 594–678. *31*

Gibson, E. J. (1969) *Principles of Perceptual Learning and Development*. New York: Appleton-Century-Crofts. *93, 94*

Gould, J. D. (1967) Pattern recognition and eye-movement parameters. *Perception and Psychophysics* 2: 399–407. *58, 64*

Gould, J. D. and Dill, A. B. (1969) Eye-movement parameters and pattern discrimination. *Perception and Psychophysics* 6: 311–20. *59*

Gould, J. D. and Schaffer, A. (1965) Eye-movement patterns in scanning numeric displays. *Perceptual and Motor skills 20*: 521–35. *59*

Green, D. M. and Swets, J. A. (1966) *Signal Detection Theory and Psychophysics*. New York: John Wiley. *45*

Gregory, R. L. (1966) *Eye and Brain*. London: Weidenfeld and Nicolson. *120, 122*

Gummerman, K. (1971) Selective perception and the number of alternatives. *American Journal of Psychology* 84: 173–9. *128*

Haber, R. N. (1966) The nature of the effect of set on perception. *Psychological Review 73*: 335–50. *126*

Haber, R. N. and Hershenson, M. (1973) *The Psychology of Visual Perception.* New York: Holt, Rinehart and Winston. *96, 97*

Haber, R. N. and Standing, L. G. (1970) Direct estimates of apparent duration of a flash followed by visual noise. *Canadian Journal of Psychology 24*: 216–29. *69*

Hardy, G. R. and Legge, D. L. (1968) Cross-modal induction of changes in sensory thresholds. *Quarterly Journal of Experimental Psychology 20*: 20–9. *47*

Harris, C. S. and Haber, R. N. (1963) Selective attention and coding in visual perception. *Journal of Experimental Psychology 65*: 328–33. *127*

Held, R. and Bossom, J. (1961) Neonatal deprivation and adult rearrangement: complementary techniques for analysing plastic sensory-motor co-ordinations. *Journal of Comparative and Physiological Psychology 54*: 33–7. *36*

Held, R. and Hein, A. V. (1963) Movement produced stimulation in the development of visually guided behavior. *Journal of Comparative and Physiological Psychology 56*: 872–6. *35*

Hochberg, J. (1970) Attention, organisation, and consciousness. In D. I. Mostofsky (ed.) *Attention: Contemporary Theory and Analysis.* New York: Appleton-Century-Crofts. *129*

Holding, D. H. (1975a) Sensory storage reconsidered. *Memory and Cognition 3*: 31–41. *72*

Holding, D. H. (1975b) A rejoinder. *Memory and Cognition 3*: 49–50. *72, 73*

Hotopf, W. H. N. (1966) The size-constancy theory of visual illusions. *British Journal of Psychology 57*: 307–18. *123*

Howarth, C. I. and Bloomfield, J. R. (1971) Search and selective attention. *British Medical Bulletin 27*: 253–8. *64, 74*

Hubel, D. H. and Wiesel, T. N. (1962) Receptive fields, binocular interaction, and functional architecture in the cat's visual cortex. *Journal of Physiology 160*: 106–54. *96*

Hubel, D. H. and Wiesel, T. N. (1968) Receptive fields and functional architecture of monkey striate cortex. *Journal of Physiology 195*: 215–43. *96*

Ingling, N. W. (1972) Categorization: a mechanism for rapid information processing. *Journal of Experimental Psychology 94*: 239–43. *132*

Jakobson, R., Fant G. M. and Halle, M. (1951) *Preliminaries to Speech Analysis.* Cambridge, Mass.: MIT Press. *93*

James, W. (1890) *The Principles of Psychology.* New York: Holt, Rinehart and Winston. *76*

Jonides, J. and Gleitman, H. (1972) A conceptual category

effect in visual search: O as a letter or digit. *Perception and Psychophysics 12*: 457–60. *133*

Juola, J. F., Leavitt, D. D. and Choe, C. C. (1974) Letter identification in word, nonword, and single-letter displays. *Bulletin of the Psychonomic Society 4*: 278–80. *130, 131*

Kahneman, D. (1968) Method, findings and theory in studies of visual masking. *Psychological Bulletin 70*: 404–25. *70*

Kaufman, L. and Richards, W. (1969) Spontaneous fixation tendencies for visual forms. *Perception and Psychophysics 5*: 85–8. *61*

Krendel, E. S. and Wodinsky, J. (1960) Search in an unstructured visual field. *Journal of the Optical Society of America 50*: 562–8. *64*

Kristofferson, M. W. (1972) Types and frequency of errors in visual search. *Perception and Psychophysics 11*: 325–8. *106*

Lenneberg, E. H. (1962) The relationship of language to the formation of concepts. *Synthèse 14*: 103–9. *118*

Locher, P. J. and Nodine, C. F. (1974) The role of scanpaths in the recognition of random shapes. *Perception and Psychophysics 15*: 308–14. *62*

Lockhead, G. R. (1966) Effects of dimensional redundancy on visual discrimination. *Journal of Experimental Psychology 72*: 95–104. *112*

Lockhead, G. R. (1972) Processing dimensional stimuli: a note. *Psychological Review 79*: 410–19. *113, 114, 115*

Long, E. R., Reid, L. S. and Henneman, R. H. (1960) An experimental analysis of set: variables influencing the identification of ambiguous, visual stimulus-objects. *American Journal of Psychology 73*: 553–62. *127, 128*

Mackworth, N. H. and Morandi, A. J. (1967) The gaze selects informative details within pictures. *Perception and Psychophysics 2*: 547–52. *60*

Marcel, A. J. (1970) Some constraints on sequential and parallel processing and the limits of attention. *Acta Psychologica 33*: 77–93. *110, 111*

Menzer, G. W. and Thurmond, J. B. (1970) Form identification in peripheral vision. *Perception and Psychophysics 8*: 205–9. *25, 43, 67*

Moray, N. (1959) Attention in dichotic listening: affective cues and the influence of instructions. *Quarterly Journal of Experimental Psychology 11*: 56–60. *84*

Moray, N. (1967) Where is capacity limited? A survey and a model. *Acta Psychologica 27*: 84–92. *88*

Moray, N. (1969) *Attention: Selective Processes in Vision and Hearing.* London: Hutchinson Educational. *77*

Morton, J. (1964) The effects of context upon speed of reading, eye-movements and eye-voice span. *Quarterly Journal of Experimental Psychology 16*: 340–55. *60, 61*

Neisser, U. (1963) Decision-time without reaction-time: experiments in visual scanning. *American Journal of Psychology 76*: 376–85. *104, 132*

Neisser, U. (1967) *Cognitive Psychology*. New York: Appleton-Century-Crofts. *69, 77, 100, 101, 119*

Neisser, U. and Beller, H. K. (1965) Searching through word lists. *British Journal of Psychology 56*: 349–58. *105*

Neisser, U., Novick, R. and Lazar, R. (1963) Searching for ten targets simultaneously. *Perceptual and Motor Skills 17*: 955–61. *105*

Nickerson, R. S. (1973) Can characters be classified directly as digits vs letters or must they be identified first? *Memory and Cognition 1*: 477–84. *132*

Noton, D. and Stark, L. (1971) Eye movements and visual perception. *Scientific American 224*: 34–43. *62, 63, 64, 103, 118*

Pollack, I. and Ficks, L. (1954) Information of elementary multidimensional auditory displays. *Journal of the Acoustical Society of America 26*: 155–8. *112*

Poulton, E. C. (1968) The new psychophysics: six models for magnitude estimation. *Psychological Bulletin 69*: 1–19. *52*

Pritchard, R. M. (1961) Stabilized images on the retina. *Scientific American 204*: 72–8. *56*

Rabbitt, P. M. A. (1967) Learning to ignore irrelevant information. *American Journal of Psychology 80*: 1–13. *100*

Ratliff, F. (1972) Contour and contrast. *Scientific American 226*: 91–102. *29*

Reed, S. K. (1973) *Psychological Processes in Pattern Recognition*. New York: Academic Press. *101*

Reicher, G. M. (1969) Perceptual recognition as a function of meaningfulness of stimulus material. *Journal of Experimental Psychology 81*: 275–80. *130*

Sanders, A. (1963) *The Selective Process in the Functional Visual Field*. Soesterberg, The Netherlands: Institute for Perception, RVO-TNO. *65, 66*

Selfridge, O. G. (1959) Pandemonium: a paradigm for learning. In *Mechanisation of Thought Processes*. London: HMSO. *99, 103*

Selfridge, O. G. and Neisser, U. (1960) Pattern recognition by machine. *Scientific American 203*: 60–8. *99*

Shiffrin, R. M. and Grantham, D. W. (1974) Can attention be allocated to sensory modalities? *Perception and Psychophysics 15*: 460–74. *88, 89*

Snyder, H. L. (1973) Dynamic visual search patterns. In *Visual*

Search. Washington, DC: NAS–NRC Committee on Vision. *61*

Sperling, G. (1960) The information available in brief visual presentations. *Psychological Monographs 74*. *68, 69*

Sperling, G. (1963) A model for visual memory tasks. *Human Factors 5*: 19–31. *70*

Sperling, G. (1967) Successive approximations to a model for short-term memory. *Acta Psychologica 27*: 285–92. *70*

Stacey, B. and Pike, R. (1970) Apparent size, apparent depth and the Müller-Lyer illusion. *Perception and Psychophysics 7*: 125–8. *123*

Steinman, R. M., Haddad, G. M., Skavenski, A. A. and Wyman, D. (1973) Miniature eye movement. *Science 181*: 810–19. *56*

Sternberg, S. (1966) High-speed scanning in human memory. *Science 153*: 652–4. *106, 119*

Sternberg, S. (1975) Memory scanning: new findings and current controversies. *Quarterly Journal of Experimental Psychology 27*: 1–32. *106*

Stevens, S. S. (1961) The psychophysics of sensory functions. In W. A. Rosenblith (ed.) *Sensory Communication*. Cambridge, Mass.: MIT Press. *50, 52*

Stevens, S. S. (1966) A metric for the social consensus. *Science 151*: 530–41. *53*

Stevens, S. S. (1971) Issues in psychophysical measurement. *Psychological Review 78*: 426–50. *49*

Stratton, G. M. (1896) Some preliminary experiments on vision without inversion of the retinal image. *Psychological Review 3*: 611–17. *35*

Sutherland, N. F. (1973) Object recognition. In E. C. Carterette and M. P. Friedman (eds) *Handbook of Perception, Vol. III*. New York: Academic Press. *102*

Taylor, M. M., Lindsay, P. M. and Forbes, S. M. (1967) Quantification of shared capacity processing in auditory and visual discrimination. *Acta Psychologica 27*: 223–9. *88*

Townsend, J. T. (1971) A note on the identifiability of parallel and serial processes. *Perception and Psychophysics 10*: 161–3. *108*

Treisman, A. M. (1964a) The effect of irrelevant material on the efficiency of selective listening. *American Journal of Psychology 77*: 533–46. *82*

Treisman, A. M. (1964b) Selective attention in man. *British Medical Bulletin 20*: 12–16. *84, 103*

Treisman, A. M. and Geffen, G. (1967) Selective attention and cerebral dominance in perceiving and responding to speech messages. *Quarterly Journal of Experimental Psychology 19*: 1–17. *85, 86, 87*

Treisman, A. M. and Riley, J. G. A. (1969) Is selective attention selective perception or selective response? A further test. *Journal of Experimental Psychology* 79: 27–34. *87*

Uhr, L. (1966) (ed.) *Pattern Recognition*. New York: John Wiley. *99*

Uttal, W. R. (1971). The psychobiological silly season, or what happens when neurophysiological data become psychological theories. *Journal of General Psychology 84*: 151–66. *96*

Warren, R. M. (1973) Quantification of loudness. *American Journal of Psychology 4*: 807–25. *52*

Wertheimer, M. (1958) Principles of perceptual organization. In D. C. Beardslee and M. Wertheimer (eds) *Readings in Perception*. Princeton, NJ: Van Nostrand. *26, 110*

Westheimer, G. H. (1954) Eye movement responses to a horizontally moving visual stimulus. *Archives of Ophthalmology* 52: 932–43. *57*

Williams, L. G. (1966) The effect of target specification on objects fixated during visual search. *Perception and Psychophysics 1*: 315–18. *59, 64*

Woodworth, R. S. (1938) *Experimental Psychology*. New York: Holt. *68*

Woodworth, R. S. and Schlosberg, H. (1954) *Experimental Psychology* (2nd edn). New York: Holt, Rinehart and Winston. *67*

Yarbus, A. L. (1967) *Eye Movements and Vision*. New York: Plenum Press. *59, 62*

Subject Index